Scotland:
An Arranged Marriage

SCOTLAND:
AN ARRANGED MARRIAGE

J.A. PATRINA

The Author, Joe Patrina, is a singer/songwriter based in Connecticut. As with his songwriting, Joe applies his seasoned observational skills and to-the-point writing style to pen insightful works on sports, history, politics, medicine, music, and law.

Copyright © 2019 by J.A. Patrina.

All rights reserved. No part of this book may be reproduced in any form or by any electronic or mechanical means, including information storage and retrieval systems, without permission in writing from the publisher, except by reviewers, who may quote brief passages in a review.

ISBN: 978-1-7330672-8-7 [Paperback Edition]

Printed and bound in The United States of America.
Published by LittleHouse Enterprises Inc.

CONTENTS

Inroduction 1

Part I: Beginnings

Beginnings – The Land 18
Beginnings – People 27
Beginnings – The Clans 38
Beginnings – Kings of Scotland 44

Part II: Highlanders

Highlanders – Loch Ness 63
Highlanders – Torridon 69

Part – III: The Sea

Skye, Islay, Whisky & Clan Donald 103
Homeward Bound 126

Part – IV: Photos

Introduction

Upon arrival at Edinburg airport, my daughter Cody points to the car rental sign assuming it our next stop.

Daughter: *Dad, the rental cars are this way.*

Joe: *We're taking cabs into the city. We'll pick up the van when we leave for the country.*

Being a family of six with eight bags, we hire two cabs, both drivers in their 50's, both greeting us with gregarious dispositions. *En route* I chat endlessly with my totally Scottish driver, a man who can surely spar with anyone on earth about anything, and suddenly we pull up to *Prestonfield House Hotel* a magnificent 600-year old property sitting on 20 acres, set inside the gates of Edinburgh.

After the unloading of bags, watching my family disappear through the house's grand entrance, I turn to pay both fares. But the drivers seem keen to joke around with me, enjoying a bit of banter with an American.

Prestonfield House - Tara

One of the drivers inquires as to my surname. I can tell what he's thinking …

Joe: *The name is Patrina. I have a bit of Italian in me, but my wife is half Scottish.*

Driver 1 (pointing to the other driver) *Well, he's half Scottish.*

Driver 2 (pointing back at driver 1) *And he's only half Scottish as well! So there you have it.*

Edinburg, with its castle in the distance.

We all burst out laughing, not clear as to the actual joke. I pay them and off they go still chuckling to themselves.

Piper at the gate of Edinburg Castle

I suppose that no one is truly Scottish anymore, with everyone in Scotland speaking English, embracing English mores, the Gaelic language modestly spoken only in the Western Highlands.

And anyway, the Scotts descend from a combined heritage ... a troublesome marriage of Indigenous "Ice Age" People, Celtic Picts, Britons & Scotch Irish, Engels from Denmark, Norsemen from Norway and Normans from France, a churning that took place centuries ago. Maybe there is no such thing as a Scott.

Hmm ... I wonder who, beside myself, wants to explore the roots of this story?

I first came to know Scotland in the 1950's, through the *You Are There* TV show, hosted by Walter Cronkite, a favorite show of mine, that recreated historical dramas.

One episode dealt with the last Scottish attack on English soil, an attempt by the clans and *Bonnie Prince Charlie* (their "Pretend" Monarch) to regain Scottish sovereignty.

Collectively Charlie (on horseback) and his followers were called Jacobites – a political movement to put Stuart kings back onto the throne of an independent Scotland.

The term "Jacobites" stems from the Latin root of "James", as in the King James Stuarts I & II of England, who were Scottish (more to come).

Back in the 1950's I remember recognizing the English red coat uniforms (even on black and white TV) as being the same as the guys who fought Washington in the American Revolution, allowing me to guess correctly as to the approximate time frame of this Scottish *You Are There* moment – the 1700's.

The French, who encouraged Jacobites against their common enemy England – a partnership called "*The Auld Alliance*" -, sent spies into London to gage the pro-Jacobean, anti-English-King sentiment boiling beneath the surface of both English and Scottish minds.

When the French spies deemed the moment ripe, the French sent Bonnie Prince Charlie – an actual Stuart who was hiding out in Paris - over to the Scottish Highlands in 1745 with a cache of guns, to spark the long awaited insurrection.

The Scottish Highlander clans responded with all they were worth, marching with Charlie into England itself, dressed in kilts, lugging swords, shields and French supplied guns, to terrify the British.

Charlie on the march

An enraged English king sent The Duke Of Cumberland (his #3 son) north to stem the invasion, along with England's staid but disciplined army. In the *You Are There*, TV episode, the English pursue the clans "without prejudice" back into Scotland, killing all stragglers.

And the English did not stop at Hadrian's Wall - the historical border between England and Scotland, built by the Roman Emperor Hadrian 1,500 years back (see below).

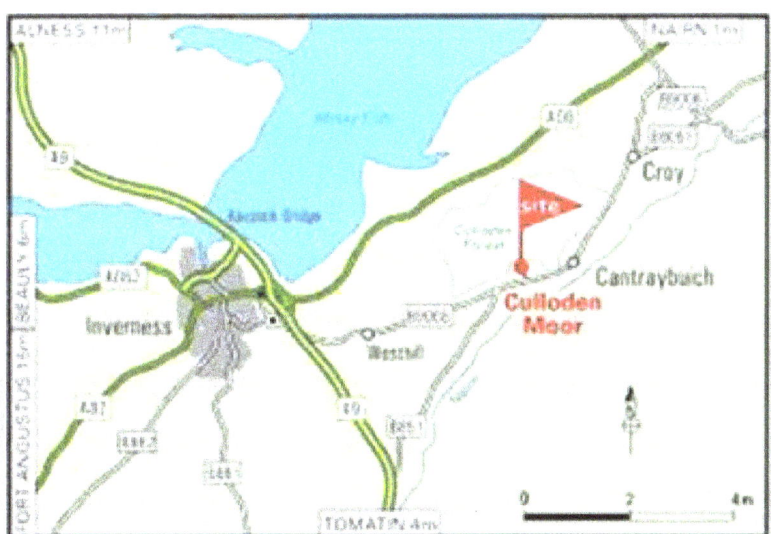

This time, in the 1700's, the motivated red coats hounded the audacious invaders all the way to the top of Scotland, unleashing one last devastating blow against the Scotts at Culloden Moor, outside of Inverness, just north of Loch Ness.

Thousands of clansmen die, leaving many women, children, boys and old men behind, hidden away deep inside of the impenetrable glens (valleys) of the Western Highlands. The English soon hunt them down, hanging many.

Later in life I heard this "*Scottish Rising*" episode referred to as "*The '45*" by modern Scotts, "*The '45*" taking place starting in 1745, and coming to a close (for ever) in 1746 - at *Culloden Moor*.

Yet even at that hostile juncture, as we will see, a multi-century marriage had already been consummated, through interbreeding between Picts, Britons, Irish, Norse, Engel and Norman bloodlines.

For a thousand years, this problematic marriage coalesced, shuffling Scott sympathies amongst those loyal to various Clan Chiefs, Scottish and English Kings. For instance, at Culloden, multiple "Lowland" Scottish regiments participated on the English side.

After Culloden, in 1746, the Duke of Cumberland sent word to his father the King, describing the total victory, asking what to do next. The King answered that he, the king, was an old man, that the Duke might soon be king; and so, the Duke should decide for himself what to do with the two thousand year old threat to mother England posed by irrepressible Scottish heathens.

The Duke Of Cumberland – the #3 Crown Prince of England – quickly decided to transform Scotland altogether, and began a systematic genocide program to kill and/or export Highlanders. The program continued for 50 more years, led by local nobles, like, Elizabeth, Countess of Sutherland (later made a duchess), who helped clear Scotland of half its population, turning the glens into vast sheep farms. Over time, the Scottish numbers dropped from 4 million to 2 million, where they remain today.

Sutherland, the northern tip of Scotland, called Sutherland by the Norwegians, simply as it lay south of Norway on their Scandinavian-centric map, is still called Sutherland today, though the Scotts do not think fondly of the Duchess herself.

Off to Australia, Nova Scotia and principally to the American Carolinas two million Scotts went – the English called it "The Clearings": people cleared to provide room for sheep, with wool a prized commodity back then as cotton was not yet king.

In Carolina, English colonists react furiously at having savage Scotts dumped upon them. The new comers, filthy, starving, and speaking Gaelic, are shunned and beaten, banished to the Appalachian Mountains further west on the edge of Indian Territory. And in these remote, mountain outposts, they stay, hiding from the English world, their Gaelic customs, whiskey and music percolating untouched for a few more centuries.

Over time the Scotch immigrants adopt English through interaction with the Americans around them, and their music evolves too. Some, like Andrew Carnegie in the 1800's, even make it big out in the world of English WASPs.

Known as hillbillies up until modern times, the American Scotch/Irish (more on the whole Scotch/Irish phenomenon later in the book) finally emerge as part of mainstream America, their culture becoming the bedrock of American folk, bluegrass, country and rockabilly musical formats.

Considering my path in life, immersed in music since the 1950's at the age of seven, then morphing into songwriting only after meeting and being "mentored" by Jeanette Carter in the 1990's (Jeanette, of the famous "Hillbilly" Carter Family clan), and considering my half-Scottish wife and quarter-Scottish children, my affection for things Scottish runs deep.

36 million Americans claim Scottish decent.

Yet before tackling this book, I would travel to Scotland many times before writing of its secrets. Read on, and you will discover what I have learned.

8

Part I – Beginnings

Beginnings - Culloden Moor – 1746

"The spirited princely youth would rouse thousands when he raised the pipe and satin banner."

Before digging deeper into the many dimensions of Scotland, I first want to cover the Culloden Moor Battle of 1746, as this pivotal event marks the demise of "the original Scotland".

Inverness (above), the capitol of the Highlands, today with 76,000 souls, sits right above the famous Loch Ness (its monster covered soon). The Loch Ness waters escape the loch and flow down the River Ness through the center of Inverness (meaning river ness), into the salt waters of the ocean.

A few miles east of the city lays *Culloden Moor Battlefield*, where *Bonnie Prince Charlie's* clan army was slaughtered.

Each time in Scotland I go to the battlefield, and my response is always the same: *grim*: not just because of the slaughter - 1,500 clansmen killed in four minutes – but due to the end of an entire civilization, that of the Highlander Clans, a civilization that like myself valued unfettered liberty above all.

A few clicks further east of the battlefield sits *Culloden House*, an architectural masterpiece born hundreds of years ago, owned by the *Forbes* family, briefly taken over by *Bonnie Prince Charlie* as his head quarters leading up to the Culloden battle, and now a five-star hotel, an oasis awaiting me, as it has done numerous times before, and we will cover the house first.

Driving all the way from Edinburgh on the wrong side of the road – for a whole day – in a 9-passenger VW mini across Scotland, through Perth, through the Trossach Mountains, through Glen Coe, and up along Loch Ness for many, many miles... I just needed the journey to end.

Tomorrow is battlefield day, and I can barely wait, except for one thing. Today is "get me to the house" day.

When last at Culloden House fourteen years prior, my son *Joseph*, at the time, was near two-years of age and we have a perfect picture of him with his older sister *Jolene*, standing on the Culloden House front lawn. One objective on this trip: to recreate that photo, but with the subjects now 16 and 18 of age respectively.

Pulling up the extended driveway I momentarily bask in the elegance of the house, and drive up to the front door receiving area.

Two gentlemen butlers - both around 50+ years of age - surface to dispatch the luggage.

Once inside, I converse with the receptionist, and hand the keys she gives me for our three rooms to my children and my wife. They escape to the rooms, me to the lounge, and the house's prized whiskey collection.

Looking over the bottles, I explain to the butler the extent of my journey and he replies:

Then it is best to get two or three into you before dinner.

I agree wholeheartedly, select as my opening choice, a bottle from *Islay* (a western Scottish island, once the seat of the Mac Donald empire – described later), and ask the chap to pick the number two and number three whiskey selections for me.

This done, we begin to chat, right as the second butler enters the room, seemingly keen to join in. I tell them about our photo plan, and the 14-year span since the last visit.

Butler #1: *We were both with the house back then; undoubtedly we have meet previously.*

Myself: *No doubt. And prior to that my wife and I were here when the owners had a pair of Collies that sat on either side of the main door, two fabulous blond Collies. This was decades ago, before we had children.*

Butler #2: *Sir, to admit, we were with the house then as well, having served for nearly 30 years.*

Butler #1: *Yes and one of those dogs never liked me; there was friction daily. Don't miss them a-toll.*

Myself: *Then we are colleagues of sort; I am glad to see you both again, though we obviously do not remember each other after so much time.*

Butler #2: *And sir, should you ever return, let us all hope that we (pointing to himself and butler #1) have safely retired.*

This results in warm laughs all around. At that point the family arrives for a round of champagne, and I go upstairs for a quick shower before dinner.

Culloden House itself evolved over time. Four hundred years ago it appeared a square box. In the

1800's the house was beautifully transformed; two smaller boxes added on either side of the big box, connected to the original box via hallway passages.

To smooth the look out, the three boxes and the passages were fronted via an overall Georgian stone façade "that is to die for".

As a refresher: in 1746, when the final Jacobean clan battle with the English was about to take place, the Scotts had just been chased out England, having dared invade it, and the Duke Of Cumberland, the King's son was closing in on them.

Culloden House, owned by a Forbes - a Scottish merchant from Inverness and a Scot loyal to the English King – would become part of Scottish history.

Forbes, a man of influence, tried to do what he could before the whole '45 thing got started, attempting to calm things down amongst the local

Front steps after dinner – the similes are a bit munch, don't you think?

clans, but his efforts paled against their fever to follow Prince Charlie to the end, no matter what. After all, this, to the clans, appeared the last stand; with liberty at stake, for a people who for a thousand years espoused the ideal of "live free or die".

And so, despite his efforts to talk clan leaders down, the 1745/6 episodes instead fell right into Forbes' lap. The retreating clansmen, coming up from northern England, seized Forbes" house – Culloden House – to give Prince Charlie a place to stay right before the coming battle.

Apparently, the last Forbes who owned the place went bankrupt, and the house eventually was bought and turned into the manor house hotel it is today. The house endures; we come and go.

A fine dinner, a good night's rest and a hot bath the next morning, and yesterday's long journey settles, just a memory.

Next, battlefield-visit-day arrives, and off we go from the house in our VW van. Years ago, Bonnie Prince Charlie, above, leaving on horseback, left here to face the actual battle. And yes, he was Bonnie, indeed.

Fourteen years back we were "it" – meaning no one else was at the old battlefield except us, my wife and kids, my mother and father, and my brother Jim, his wife and kids.

Fourteen years later, as we pull into the battlefield grounds, a new visitor center building rises from the earth blocking all views of the battlefield itself, and the parking lot hosts tour busses waiting patiently.

Oh well. Times change.

Thankfully one can still walk directly onto the battlefield through a gate attached to the new visitor center, without payment, and more so, without forced passage through the visitor center itself. Evidently, all of the tour bus tourists were inside the visitor center; no one on the battlefield itself.

The battle underway. The Duke of Cumberland, in the foreground, led the king's troops to victory.

Now it is how I remembered it.

We are on the British side of the battlefield. Some historians do not like to say "British", as that implies a strict British/Scottish conflict, and as already pointed out, the "British" side had three Scottish regiments amongst their ranks.

Instead the historians call the British forces "Government" forces, there to put down the unruly, murdering criminals: aka the clansmen.

Ok, so I am on the "Government" line, which is flying "British" flags, and 400 yards away are the clans, flying the blue "Scottish" flags, representing the criminals.

Those 1,500 clansmen who died in just four minutes … well here is how it happened:

A ways back, the clans devised a tactic called "the all out clan charge", designed to terrorize opposing troops. This ferocious onslaught had worked many times.

One has to envision the typical clansman; rough, fast, uneducated, carrying many concealed knives, able to throw an axe from 20 feet, having the axe blade rotate to split your head open, carrying swords and shields for close combat – not to mention French supplied pistols - and fearing their chief more than their enemy.

So the clans try the charge again (and why not), but not immediately, though suddenness was the key to the maneuver.

Laura, family in back, along the British line

Instead, Prince Charlie for reasons unknown, on this frigid, howling April day, ignores the advice of his generals, and personally takes charge of his 5,000 strong Jacobite army against the seasoned British army of 10,000 ... yet he waits to give the charge order.

During this delay, British cannon take out the Scottish cannon, 400 yards away. When finally Charlie gives the order, the clansmen charge without artillery support, essentially naked, across the soaking wet moorland. Conversely as they sprint, every British weapon releases multiple rounds of metal into the rampaging, Scottish horde.

Some Scotts actually reach the British line, and a hundred Brits fall in due course, but the slaughter, and the proportions of casualties – 25 to 1 – approach the numbers Julius Caesar achieved against the Celtics 1700 years earlier.

Joe, children and the only remaining battlefield structure

And then the British cavalry surfaces, previously hidden out of sight, cutting off retreat. Prince Charlie escapes as the battle disintegrates.

With a 30,000 pound sterling reward on his head, Charlie "The Pretender King" flees across Scotland to the island of Skye, and is never turned in by any Scot along the way, finally escaping back to France, where he pursues a carnal life in Paris before dying in Rome, buried by his brother, a bishop, in Saint Peters Basilica (Yikes!!!).

We walk the whole battlefield, read mass grave stone inscriptions - markers of the victims of his arrogance - and begin to walk off, my own countenance as grim as can be.

Looking up, my eyes meet two strapping, redheaded motorcyclists in bike gear coming onto the field. They read my look, and gesture solidarity, reflecting who they are: *Jacobites!*

Aye lades so am I

BEGINNINGS – THE LAND

The land and the people of Scotland are one. As described in the coming chapters, though the land formed tens of millions years before the first humans stepped upon it, once combined, both forces carved each other's destiny.

I don't know how scientists could know this, but the claim is that Scotland, the land, was once part of North America. It broke off from the American shelf and drifted south and east, eventually coming north, crashing into the European shelf above England, causing massive upheaval, new mountain ranges and volcanoes that raged for centuries.

Today, if one goes to the west of Scotland, there will be no doubt that this is exactly what happened.

One amazing claim is that the new landmass coming in from America collided with the European shelf, more or less, right where Hadrian's Wall was built. The ancient geographical border – a fault line - appropriately underpins the border wall later established by the Romans, once they gave up trying to conquer the northern Pict tribes.

When gawking at Scotland's geographical wonders, one should visualize that these formations took hold hundreds of millions of years ago.

In contrast, the Alps, according to geologists, surfaced just two million years ago, hence the Alps remain rugged, the Scottish mountains rounded by time and countless ice ages.

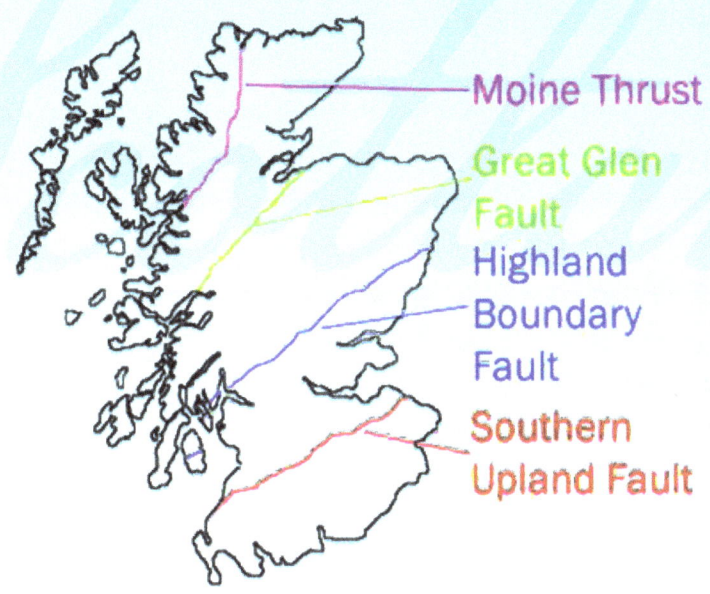

With all of the geological violence that took place, the impact area is massive.

The Highlands, in the north and west of Scotland, run for a few hundred miles, creating 150,000 square miles of wilderness, and the islands off the coast join in as an additional part of the volcanic past.

These magnificent islands are grouped as follows:

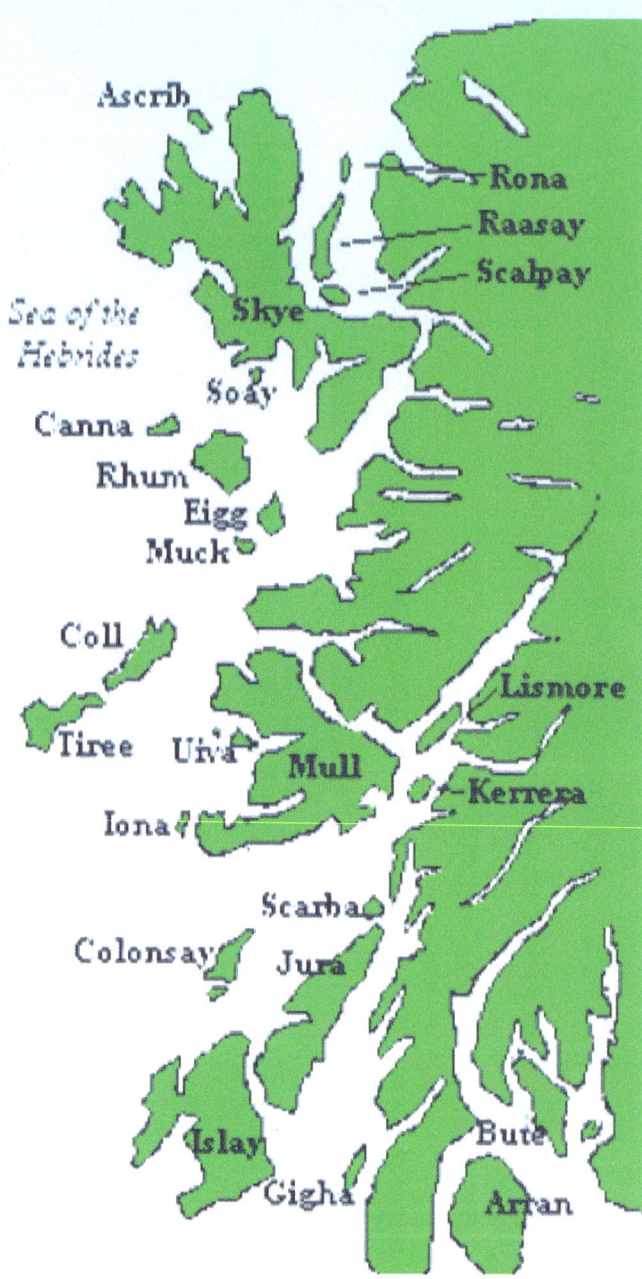

The Northern Islands – Orkney, Shetland

The Inner Hebrides (shown here) – Arran, Skye, Rum, Eigg, Mull and Islay, etc.

The Outer Hebrides – Summer Isles, Harris, Lewis & Kilda

Island life means solitude and cold wet 8-month winters.

The St Kilda islands, for example, the furthest U.K. outpost into the deep Atlantic, stayed inhabited for two thousand years by a Celtic population of merely 200, with marriage partners gleaned from the nearby Lewis and Harris islands. In 1930 the remnant people were removed from the island due to illness.

The Kilda islands have 1,000-foot cliffs, home to millions of sea birds, to which men once descended on horsehair ropes to harvest eggs. It is said that a young fellow could not marry until he wove a rope adequate to weather the harvesting perils – no widows allowed on Kilda!

BTW, the St Kilda image of these fiercely independent peoples inspired the lyric in my song *Scotland* as follows:

Well those souls on the outer islands, they let freedom ring.
Cold rain coming down forever, August takes everything

Huge mountains and breathtaking seaside cliffs reside on each of these essentially tree-less islands; Skye, alone, has 12 peaks, *The Black Cullins (see photo)*, of over 3,000 feet that rise out of the ocean up into the clouds.

Still, as inspiring as the islands are, the mainland geographical structures are even bolder, with many mountains soaring over 4,000 feet, snow holding on even in August – mount Nevis at 4,500 feet the highest.

Yet the Highland mountains offer something more – the glens. These narrow, deep and spooky valleys sit right above sea level, draining waters coming down from the respective mountain pairs sitting on each side of the glen's floor.

Here, in the glens, the clans dwelt – in isolation, living hard, living free for almost a thousand years.

To get around, footpaths ran down each glen, cutting through peat bogs, heather outcroppings, forest glades, and running aside inland lakes.

Loch Ness, the most famous of these entrapped lakes, is 21 miles long, a mile wide, over 700 feet deep, its surface sitting 50 feet above sea level; it holds more fresh water then all the lakes in England and Wales combined.

In some of the glens, footpaths (some still used today) were eventually improved to allow carts, but the first paved roads in these wilderness areas were carved out only after World War II.

Even today, most paved roads offer just one tract to drive upon, with little paved extensions available every so often, so that cars coming at each other can navigate past the other.

And, there are no straight lines anywhere.

One more thing to know: Doggerland.

"Once upon a time", Britain was attached to mainland Europe; historians call the landmass *Doggerland*, and evidence of it is regularly dredged up in the English Channel.

Towards the end of the last ice age, while massive ice sheets still remained further north, sea levels remained low due to the amount of seawater still trapped in the northern ice, which in turn, caused additional land extensions in what are now coastal areas.

According to Geologists, the last ice age lasted over 100,000 years, peaking around 22,000 years ago, with ice sheets miles high. Personally, I calculate the ice age but a few hundred years following Noah's flood around 2,400 BC.

Doggerland had its moment in the sun bringing fauna, animals and people into Britain, then disappearing into the rising oceans around 2,000 BC, leaving England, Ireland and Scotland still standing.

Abandoned homes on St Kilda. Sometimes the land wins. The same Kilda homes back in the day.

Ok, so that's "the skinny" on the land; next, let's see about the people, the clans and the kings.

BEGINNINGS – PEOPLE

Determining the age of things is a tedious business. The known tool is carbon 14 measurement. The science of this claims that living things – made of carbon 12 - also accumulate extremely rare and unstable carbon 14 molecules while eating and breathing, and when dead, the unstable carbon decays at a fixed rate, eventually disappearing altogether. Carbon 14 decays completely after 50,000 years. Anything older is sheer guesswork. With that said, let's look at what science claims.

As described in the previous chapter, they say that when the last ice age retreated, animals and humans migrated north as mosses, grasses, shrubs and trees re-established themselves on the raw, barren land, recently scraped clean by vast, mile high glaciers.

Assuming this the case, the suggestion that humans inhabited the British Isles since 3,000 BC is plausible, as that beginning comes after a few thousand years of reseeding and animal migration, and falls in the heart of the Doggerland era.

The early Scottish people, the ones dwelling there from 2,200 BC to 1,000 BC, are the ones who built all those stone things – like Stonehenge.

Assuming these people were there for 2,000 years before Julius Caesar arrived in 55 BC, one can visualize that this expanse of time equals the time from Caesar until modern times. The bible claims that one of Noah's grandsons - Gomer – migrated to the British Isles after the 2,400 BC flood. The old name for the Welsh language is Gomeraeg.

Ring of Brodgar, Orkney Island

Joseph in the heart of a cairn

To celebrate Stone Age Scotland, the family visits the Clava Cairns – a burial site located four miles from Culloden Battlefield (Cairn and magic standing stone photos follow).

Standing Stones

While rough time frames may be known, no one knows much about the racial makeup of these early British occupiers. There are no fossils, carbon 14 markers - no nothing – just stones. But people were on the land, and the one's up north, undoubtedly established a base bloodline for the Scotts, thousands of years before the Celts arrived.

The Celtics, a relatively "modern" people, are also mysterious. It is said that Celtics, for some time before 1200 BC, resided in middle Europe – Switzerland/Austria/ Czechoslovakia – and around 1,000 BC, spread west and north into Spain, France, Belgium and finally Britannia. During this expansion, Germanic people stayed north of the Celts, becoming longstanding adversaries, but the fate of the original 'stone" people who once lived in the new Celtic-conquered territories stays unknown – extermination and interbreeding are the two possibilities.

When the Celtics came into Britannia, they came as tribes, some going to Ireland, some scattered around England, Cornwall and Wales, and one tribe – The Picts – occupying the faintly habitable land of Scotland, the lowland areas east and north of the western highlands. (The Romans called them Picts, i.e. pictured/tattooed people).

The highland region, too rugged to support life, remained relatively empty of human concentration for centuries.

And so, settled in the gentler lands, the Picts lived their lives, probably mixing with indigenous people. For generation after generation this boutique mixed race lived in relative solitude, until, one day, the Romans arrived.

Julius Caesar first stepped foot in Britain in 55 BC, but did not stay long, though he killed many of the blue-painted Celts who stood up to him.

The Romans eventually came in for keeps, and worked their way north, eventually reaching Pict territory, getting no further. Many Roman attempts to subdue the Picts transpired, including the time the Roman #9 legion was nearly wiped out by these northern, semi-bronze age heathens who spoke a funny language (the Romans said the Pictish, Gaelic language was different from the Gaelic language of other Celts across the islands. My guess, the Picts merged – genetically and culturally - with the indigenous people, whereas most Celtic tribes in the south maintained solidarity with their bloodline.

In 122 AD, the Emperor Hadrian had enough of the Picts and ordered a wall built (*below*). Hadrian's Wall served as a symbol of a two-way truce; you stay on your side and we will stay on our side. It worked.

Rome officially fell in 408 AD, when Alaric pillaged the city of Rome itself. Those Romans living in Britain either left, or mixed with the Celtics still there, with Celtic kings, like Arthur, establishing footholds for themselves. Invading peoples soon filled the vacuum created by Rome's demise.

From 400 AD onward, the so-called Anglo/Saxon peoples poured into Britain.

These came in from what is now Denmark, and the Jutes were also part of the invasion.

Angles, is also spelled as "Engels", which makes more sense as this "E" variation is the root for "England".

One can see the displacement of the Celts (Britons) due to the invasion. The King Arthur legend comes from the Saxon onslaught in the southwest (*bottom left*), with Arthur holding onto that last bit of turf, now called Cornwall.

Also invading at this time were the Irish, who slipped in between the Stratheclyde Britons and the northern Picts.

The "Scotch Irish" (as these Irish were subsequently called) took a few of the islands, plus the rugged highland territory no one particularly wanted, with the Picts holding on to the good land to the north and east.

But once in proximity of each other, the two bodies of Irish and Pictish Celts co-existed well enough, though the Scotch Irish culture ultimately dominated, with the Pictish language and identity ultimately fading away.

Similarly, in the same time frame, in Northumbria, below Hadrian's Wall, the Engel identity gave way to Saxon dominance (Yet it is the Engels of whom England is named).

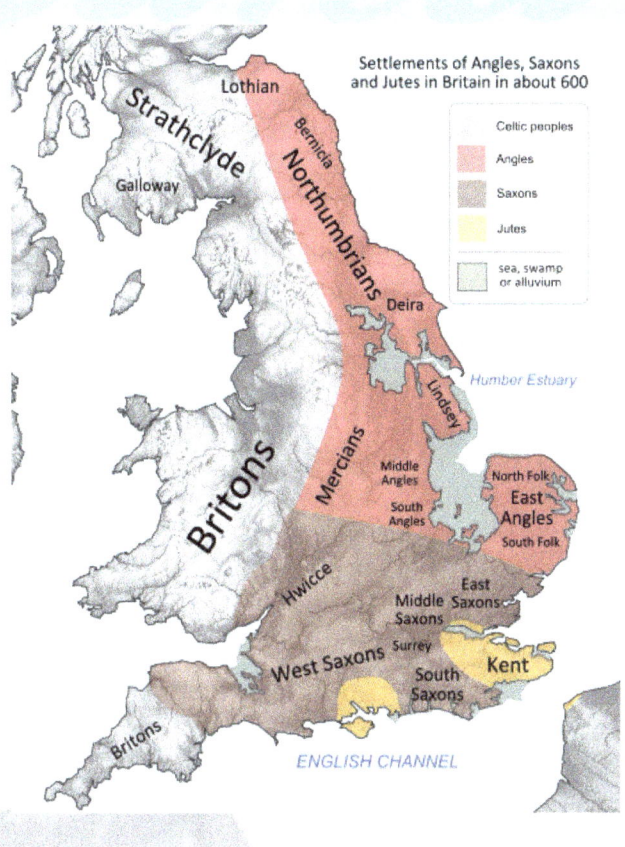

But as all of this Celtic mixing simmered in Scotland, and the Engel/Saxon/Jute tribes were working out their new kingdoms further south, a new invader, the Vikings, appeared around 800 AD. These Norwegians took the Scottish islands starting with the Orkneys and Shetlands up north, later populating the Outer and Inner Hebrides and some of the mainland coast as well.

Today, as we travel the coastal areas and islands, I look place names up, and their source is sometimes Gaelic and sometimes Norse. For instance, the English word "anchor" is "ancaire in Gaelic and "akkeri" in Norse, a real chicken-and-egg puzzle.

On this map (next page), circa 900 AD, one can see a) the Norse coastal areas loyal to Norway, b) Scotia, a new kingdom of Scotch Irish and Picts who merged under King Kenneth MacAlpin in 834 AD to defend against the Norse, c) the Strathclyde Celts, d) Northumbrian Engels, and e) Morey, the last Pict kingdom. Morey, of Shakespeare's King Macbeth fame, would be pulled into greater Scotia in the 1100's.

When the Norsemen arrived, some genocide against the Scotch Irish living on the islands transpired, but many people born of this territory in the 1100's claim both Celtic and Norse bloodlines, the most

33

important example being a certain Celtic chief named *Somerled (summer wanderer)*, patriarch of the MacDonald Clan and self-proclaimed *First Lord Of The Islands*. Somerled's decedents would rule the Islands and some of the Highlands for the next 350 years until around 1450 AD.

One should ponder the above. First, this area of Scotland was actually populated by a hybrid of Irish/Norwegians who we now call Scottish, and second, these Hybrid people ruled as masters of their own world for 350 years, 100 years longer than the United States has been in existence. This streak of independence would not fade away easily, and ultimately would be rooted out via genocide, after Culloden in the 1700's (more on the Mac Donald empire later).

So that is what took place in the Irish parts of Scotland during the "dark ages". Pictish Scotland experienced a different path in those years. In the east, there seems to have been mingling amongst the old Pict and Engel families, as many lowland Scottish names are even today quite English sounding.

In any event, this area of Scotland produced the first Scottish Kings, who at first operated out of Stirling Castle. The fortified town of Stirling still sits at the "crossing Point" of the Forth River. Viking ships, for example, wanting to penetrate further into Scotland, could sail up stream only this far, and would need to cross over on foot to get past Stirling.

Stirling Castle below

Things were going fine in the Scottish Kingdom for a time until in 1066 William, Duke of Normandy, sailed across the English Channel, and defeated King Harold Godwinson, the Saxon king, at the *Battle of Hastings* (Blonde Harold (below) was shot in the eye with an arrow).

Besides ushering in a long era of French/Norman rule in England, the Normans affected Scotland as well.

William was a complete conqueror, building castles out of stone up and down England (previously, Saxon chiefs erected wood/dirt forts), and William used marriage contracts between Norman and Saxon families to weave everything together.

Well, there is something that most do not know; William used the same marriage technique to infiltrate the Scottish nobility.

Famous Scot monarchs, like Robert The Bruce, and the whole Stuart bloodline were at their core Norman. Through intermarriage, William effectively compromised the Scottish nobility for all time by causing so-called Scottish kings to betray the Scottish people for their own alliances with the English.

The most famous case in point is the betrayal of William Wallace during the *Wars of Scottish Independence* – around 1300, (Wallace - otherwise known as "Brave Heart").

Here is the kick in the head: all the major players in the brave heart saga – William Wallace, Robert the Bruce, and John Comyn - were of Norman decent: For example, Wallace's Norman French name was *William le Waleys*; Bruce's Norman name was *Robert de Bruys*.

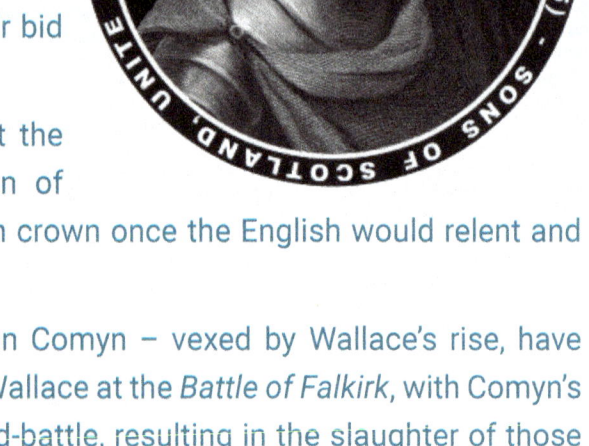

Though all three strived "for Scottish independence", Bruce needed to eliminate Wallace and Comyn, seeing them as rivals for the Scottish crown should the Scotts succeed with their bid for independence.

William Wallace, the revered victor over the English at the recent *Battle of Stirling Bridge*, was appointed "Guardian of Scotland" - the king in waiting -, poised to take the Scottish crown once the English would relent and leave Scotland.

Robert the Bruce and John Comyn – vexed by Wallace's rise, have been accused of sabotaging Wallace at the *Battle of Falkirk*, with Comyn's knights leaving the field in mid-battle, resulting in the slaughter of those remaining with Wallace. This battle gave the English King Edward I - who led his own troops, and may have cut deals with fellow Normans Comyn and Bruce before the battle - a temporary victory.

With Wallace captured, drawn and quartered in London, and Comyn murdered by Bruce, Bruce neatly proclaims himself King of Scotland. Bruce is a successful king, eventually defeating Edward II at the *Battle of Bannockburn*, keeping Scotland free of England for 20 years.

And so, the take-away from all of this is, that while Norman overlords schemed for kingdoms, the Celts in the kilts died.

Ironically, Norman infiltration of Celtic nobility via marriage cut two ways, as it resulted in a Scottish King becoming King of England.

The Scottish Stewart line came into power in the 1400 AD time frame. They were Normans, and their name stems from their job title: steward of the king's finances in Scotland. From this excellent springboard the Stewart family survived and prospered, finally becoming Kings of Scotland, changing "Stewart" to "Stuart" along the way.

James Stuart IV really hit pay dirt in 1603, when the English King died without heirs, and the closest heir was – that's right – James IV up in Scotland.

So they offered James the job of being the King of both England, and Scotland. He accepted, and a century of the worst kind of upheaval possible, fueled by religious fever, commenced in the British Isles (more on this in the Kings chapter).

A good map of how all these early years shaped Scotland's highland/lowland dichotomy – leading to the "45" and Culloden - sits below:

BEGINNINGS - THE CLANS

Clan map circa 1600

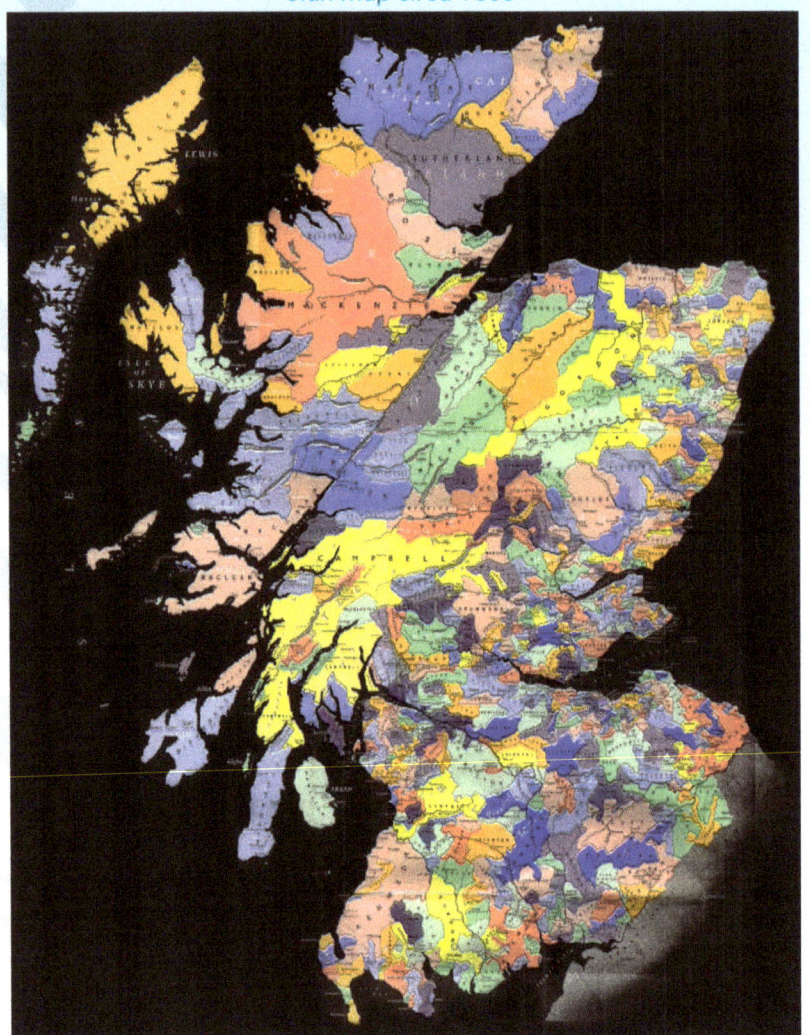

The Clans underpin Celtic culture, forming the matrix of Celtic ways. The Picts had Clans, as did the Scotch Irish, as did the Strathclyde Britons. Let's take a look...

As said in ancient Celtic times: Remember the men from whence you came. This sentiment reflects the mores of the era, where one's surname stems from the father's – as today, but with a caveat describe later.

Once upon a distant time up until, say, 1500, surnames referred to places, professions, slave status or paternal heritage. This was before America, where individuals mattered, in contrast to those more brutal times where people were categorized based upon sheer usefulness, place or parentage.

For example, the Irish used an "O" or a "Mc", to signify that an O'Brian, for instance, was a descendent of Brian Bauru (a famous Irish Chief, and the first King of all Ireland in the 900's), or that a McBride was the descendent of "Bride".

When the Irish migrated over to Scotland from 400 AD onwards, the "O" nomenclature was dropped all together, and in recent centuries the "Mc" was extended to a "Mac", for some unknown reason, so that today we have Macgregor's in our midst, and are quite pleased that this is so.

So this describes the naming apparatus of the Clan system, but there is much more to it.

The first thing to imagine is the sheer desperation of ancient peoples to just survive, and hopefully, to survive with a few base luxuries, like protecting one's wife and children from the brutality and covertness of others.

From this dread, came the system of Chiefs, not just in Scotland, but also fully throughout the emerging human race. The Chief was empowered to provide for the safety and decency of the Clan. In doing so, the Chief and his immediate family lived with benefits - hereditary benefits no less - which meant castles, tax revenues, imported goods, certain girls, executive decrees and dispute judgments as you saw fit.

As the comedy line goes "It's good to be King", or even a Chief.

But as ripe as this dynamic stood to invite excesses by the Chiefs and their immediate Kin, a balancing counterforce, the society at large, proclaimed the Clan on top, the Chief owing his allegiance to it.

Caesar, for example, wrote saying that Celtic Chiefs believed that commoners deserved protection from people in power. A Nobleman was to guarantee that no harm came to his supporters. If it does, he loses face, and falls in status. (Celtic painted bodies in the time of Ceasar).

As you will read later in the book, this longstanding Highlander societal equilibrium was eventually broken by the always clever English during the Highland Clearings era of the late 1700's. The Chiefs were bribed to betray Clan commoners, setting up sheep farms to produce wool; the commoners no longer embraced or needed.

Besides this trait of fidelity, the Celtic Clans, around for thousands of years in one form or another, lived as nature-venerating and polytheistic peoples.

So as not to be confused by terminology, the name Celt originated with the ancient Greeks, who called the barbarian peoples of central Europe Keltoi. One might hear Keltic in place of Celtic, but these labels refer to the same phenomenon.

The Roman author Strabo wrote of three Celtic specialists that held the early Clan community together: The Bards - musicians, singers, and poets, the Vates, prophets, and the Druids, religious leaders, who performed sacrifices and preached re-incarnation.

Celtics recognized many levels of supernatural beings and divinities, female as well as male, establishing shrines at springs, rivers, lakes, and in woodland settings, possessing an immense body of traditional lore, concerning nature, the seasons, astronomy, death, and transformation.

These orientations dissolved once Christianity established itself from 500 onward, with missionaries like St Patrick in Ireland and St Columba in Scotland. The Druids were gone, but belief in fairies and leprechauns prevailed.

Spirit worship

The Little People

Saint Columba Circa 500 AD

    The formerly universal community structure of the Celtic clans gradually eroded away everywhere except in the highlands of Scotland, the last holdout. From painted warriors in Caesar's day, modern, lowland Scotts became a stylish lot.

    Strictly speaking, a clan consists of the chief's family and the branches that, like the Jewish system, can prove male descent from the founder through the female line. Although this is the strict familial definition of a clan, it was rarely interpreted so rigidly, and in practice the clan includes every family that accepts the authority and protection of the local clan chief.

The Clans may have been noble in many respects, but they were sure primitive overall. Years ago, I read a quote from a British Officer who fought in both the Scottish War of 1745 & 6, and the American French & Indian War of 1765, saying that the Scottish Clansmen and the American Indians were basically equivalent in their limited breath of knowledge and in their inherent savagery. He may be right or wrong.

One thing I ponder is with such propensities for independence by the clans, it is a miracle that a Scottish Kingdom came together. It was by necessity, as follows...

The Picts and the Scotch Irish were partly unified back in the 800's by Kenneth Macalpin, a Pict, to stand against the Norsemen.

But as described earlier, it took an invasion by French Normans in 1066 to really get the idea of big kingdoms going.

With the need for kingdoms – and not just local Chiefs - to survive, by the 1700's, the Clan system had dissipated everywhere but in the highland glens, and after the Glencoe Massacre of 1692 (covered later), the last stand for the Clans would happen mid-century at Culloden Moor in 1746, and it would put the final nail in the Clan way-of-life coffin.

BEGINNINGS - KINGS OF SCOTLAND

In a book like this, which seeks to reveal "the gestalt" of Scotland (Gestalt = an organized whole that is perceived as more than the sum of its parts), I try to not overdo the details though some details are must haves. And so next, I will summarize the brutal lives of the Scottish Kings as concisely as I can (Above, Macbeth).

Keep in mind that two forces carved Scottish history, those of the Highlanders (the descendants of Scotch Irish and Norsemen), and those of the Scottish Kings (the descendants of Picts, Engels, Normans and Britons). The rise and fall of the Highlander side is covered in depth throughout the book. Here we look at the Scottish Kings, almost all destined to kill and be killed.

The timeline of Scottish Kings is complex and a practical way to understand them is required. The first Scottish King, Kenneth Macalpin came to power in 840 AD, and the last Scottish Monarch, Queen Anne, cashed in Scottish independence for good in 1702 to become Queen of a unified Great Britain, with Scotland never breaking away again. In these 900 years six families dominated the Scottish throne, and the history can be visualized as the treachery and transitions of each family "house".

HOUSE OF MACALPIN 843-1034

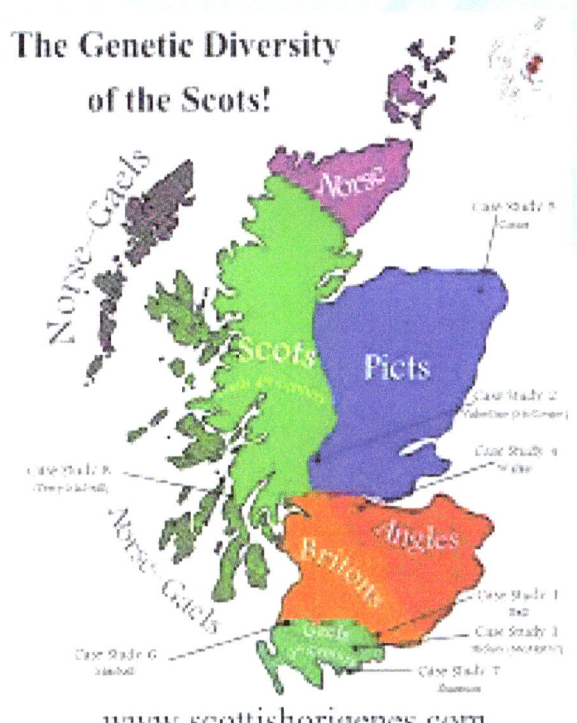

In the 800's, the Norse Vikings were on the prowl, attacking many parts of the world, including the coasts of Scotland. Both the Scotch Irish and the Picts were under constant attack, and besides occupying Sutherland and the islands, the Norse killed the heads of both Celtic groups in battle. A need for Celtics to band together resulted, and the first King of Scotland, Kenneth Macalpin, arose the perfect choice, as his father was Scotch Irish and his mother a Pict.

The new kingdom was called Scotia, but did not include Moray (some holdout Picts to the north), nor Lothian (Engel territory to the southeast), or Strathclye Celtics (the Britons to the southwest). These would be assimilated later along with Norse Sutherland and the islands.

Kenneth was crowned at Scone, near Perth in the east, in the presence of the Stone Of Scone, a red stone block that thereafter became the coronation symbol of Scottish Kings until the 1200's when it was stolen by Edward I of England, brought to Westminster Abby, London, where all subsequent English Kings (including today's Elizabeth II) were crowned in its presence.

The last Macalpin King, Malcom II, had no male offspring, only daughters, but he killed the children of his relatives so that Duncan Dunkeld, his daughter's son, could become king.

HOUSE OF DUNKELD 1034 – 1058

Duncan, the grandson, moves along nicely, having male heirs, until Macbeth, his cousin, kills Duncan in battle.

Macbeth Dunkeld (of Shakespeare fame) lasts 17 years until Malcolm Canmore, one of Duncan's sons grows up, and kills Macbeth in battle. What comes around goes around. (Above: The Stone of Scone under the King's Throne).

HOUSE OF CANMORE 1058 – 1292

This Canmore family rules Scotland for about as long as the United States has been in existence, but that doesn't mean things were "peachy". After 1066, with the Normans controlling England, many Engels flee Northumbria into the southern Lothian region of Scotland seeking alliance with the Scots. This "diaspora" of Engels into Scotland results in the melding of the English peoples in the Scottish lowlands. But the Normans are relentless, going after Scotland itself, splintering the Canmore family at every juncture.

For instance, two Canmore cousins, Donald and Edmund, take power by killing King Duncan II their uncle. But Edmund's brother Edgar brings in a Norman army to overthrow the cousins, his cousin allowed to become a monk, his brother blinded and imprisoned until death. Edgar, the new friend of the Normans, begins a pattern of intermarriage with the French Normans, yet many Canmore's, though now related to the Kings of England, fight time and again against England to hold onto Scotland for themselves. To preserve their independence, the Canmores enter into what would be known as the Auld Alliance with France, against England.

HOUSE OF BRUCE 1251- 1371

Mentioned earlier in the book, the Norman House of Bruce started with trickery and cunning.

After Edward I of England (Above) trounces the Scots, stealing the Stone of Scone, a Scottish champion arises in the form of William Wallace, who finally punches the English in the nose at the aforementioned battle of Stirling Bridge.

As Mentioned, Wallace's subsequent defeat at Falkirk at the hands of Edward I is blamed on a plot by Bruce and his partner Comyn to leave Wallace abandoned on the field of battle. Later Bruce stabs Comyn to death in a church and becomes king of Scotland, crowned at Scone, though the stone itself, just stolen by Edward the English King, now sits in Westminster Abby.

HOUSE OF STEWART 1371 - 1714

Robert The Bruce's son David II, next reins, but produces no heir, leaving the door open for the powerful Stewart family.

The Stuart dynasty - they change the spelling from Stewart to Stuart so that French supporters can pronounce the name - begins with Robert II taking the throne as King of Scots in 1371, and ends with the death of Queen Anne of Great Britain in 1714. In total, 9 Stuart monarchs rule Scotland – and sometimes England - over 343 years. When that was not enough, Stuart advocates foist Bonnie Prince Charlie, a playboy sent over from Paris, onto the Highlanders in 1745, wanting to give the Stuart family one more try.

Before becoming Kings, the Stewarts were stewards of the Kings finances for a few hundred years. They are Britons, from original Celtic tribes in the Strathclyde region of southwest Scotland. This fact matters, as besides Scotch Irish, Norsemen, Picts, Engels and Normans, The Stuarts affirm that this often forgotten bloodline, Britons, eventually has a major seat at the Scottish and world history tables. Notable Stuart monarchs follow:

Robert II, the first Stuart King – Robert is the son of a high-ranking Stewart father and the daughter of his namesake Robert The Bruce, and so, when David Bruce has no children, this Bruce/Stuart descendent, Bruce II, is instated in 1371.

Mary Queen Of Scotts – Her grandmother was an English Tudor, and this leads to her son, James, becoming next in line for the English throne in 1603. These final Scotch/English Stuarts bring about the demise of Scotland, turmoil to England and a long period of neglect within the American colonies, fostering American independence.

James I – In 1603, James was not king of one nation, but king of three separate nations: England, Wales and Scotland, thereby preserving an illusion of Scottish independence.

Charles I – James' son, is executed by parliament in 1649 for pro French sentiment, and replaced by Cromwell, a military dictator and a puritan, as the Stuart family retreats to Paris.

Oliver Cromwell – Parliament's appointed dictator, goes on to crush Catholics in Britain and Ireland.

Charles II – Upon Cromwell's death in 1660, Charles II, the son of executed Charles I and a French mother, is called back to London and restored as King of England, Wales, Scotland and, - thanks to Cromwell's prior work in depopulating half of Ireland – King of Ireland. He is called the "Merry King" for bringing debauchery back to England following the staid Cromwell era. When Charles II dies, his brother James II, a French Catholic with four illegitimate children and no heirs is instated.

James II – James Stuart II (seen above with his father Charles II), becomes the last Catholic King of England, and is in the eyes of many, just another debauched French Catholic with concubines and bastard offspring. This results in the Glorious Revolution of 1688, where James II flees England.

William Of Orange, a Dutch Protestant married to James' eldest Protestant daughter Mary, is invited into England to take the throne.   Note: William approves the Glen Coe Massacre a few years latter.

Queen Anne – William and Mary have no children, which leads to Mary's younger sister Anne, a protestant, being instated. In 1702 under Anne, who became the last Stuart monarch, the separate English, Welch, Scottish and Irish Kingdoms are unified into the Kingdom of Great Britain, with the "Union Jack" flag designed accordingly. Anne, a Stuart, puts the last nail in the Scottish coffin.

The Hanoverian King Georges I, II & III – During Anne's rein, Parliament passes a law forbidding any more Catholic Monarchs. The House of Hanover, German Protestants, is invited in to rule Great Britain, though fifty Catholic nobles have higher claims to the throne.

Bonnie Prince Charlie (Above)- In 1745 Charlie – defender of the faith - is brought in from Paris to give the Stuarts one last go, but is defeated at Culloden Moor by the Duke of Cumberland, George II's son.

Later, in 1776, English colonists in America would take their chances for independence, successfully rebelling under the leadership of George Washington of Virginia against George III of Great Britain.

And so an independent Scotland passes into history, though many Scotts today consider themselves Jacobites. Recently, in 2014, a vote for Scottish separation was taken, and the Jacobites lost, yet gaining 45% of the vote.

Up next, the Glen Coe Massacre...

Oil painting of a Mac Donald murdered at Glen Coe

Part II - Highlanders

The Glencoe Massacre of 1692

"The orders are that none be spared, nor the government troubled by prisoners."

The drive from Edinburg to Culloden features two great stretches of land: *Glencoe* and *Loch Ness* – two giant biospheres separated by Ben Nevis, Scotland's highest mountain at 4,500 feet. As you will see, the *Massacre at Glencoe,* in 1692, caused a pivot in Scottish history, and *Loch Ness* has its own famous legacy as well. So let's dig in, starting with Glencoe.

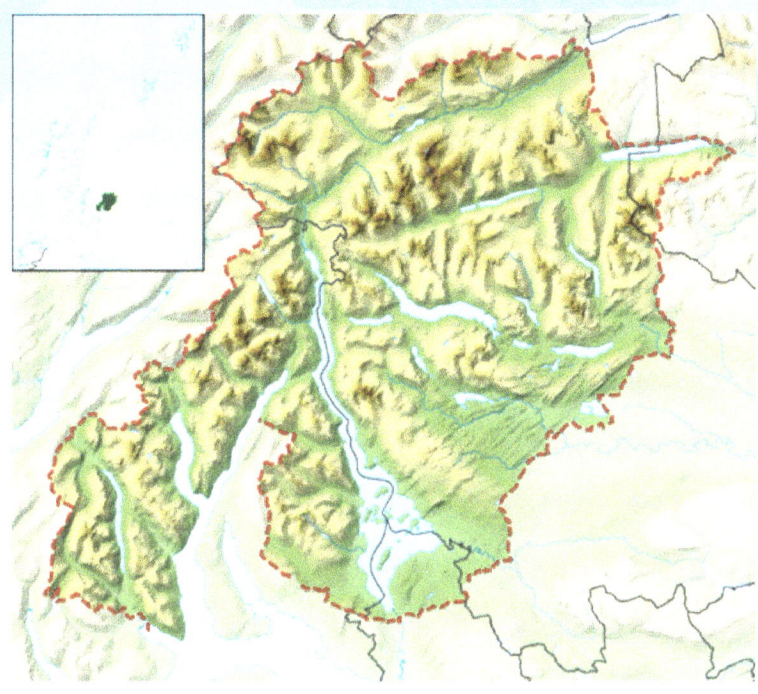

After a few hours of driving north and west of Edinburg, through lovely rolling farmland, my eyes begin to look for *The Trossachs*, the first mountain range of the highlands.

As seen on the map, this range appears a giant volcano with mountains radiating away from the center. In the valleys lie entrapped lakes, including the big one, Loch Lomond.

In the U.S. we call mountains "mountains". In Britain specific labels indicate the heights of the various mountains. *Munros* rise more than 3,000 feet, *Corbetts* more than 2,500, and so on. Perhaps 25 such labels float around the British Isles in reference to mountain sizes, with Scotland having its own nomenclature, England a separate set of names, and Ireland a separate set as well. (Trossach Munros are shown below)

The Trossachs boast 21 Munros and 19 Corbetts, plus the majesty of Loch Lomond, 24 miles long, with the greatest surface area of any lake in the U.K.; though Ness has more water due to its depth. (Above, Loch Lomond from the air)

Now we're getting somewhere, I muse, after driving hours and finally entering a mountain setting, so I figure it is time to make a family pronouncement.

I get everyone's attention; meaning ear buds leave the ears of my four "children", ages 16 to 22. Feeling like Chevy Chase I say:

These mountains are the Trossachs. They separate the highlands from the lowlands. Once on the other side we will travel down the Glencoe valley for 40 miles or so until Fort William. In Fort William, we can stop at Inverlochy Castle for tea.

For now, what you need to know is that by direct order of the King, a British military unit murdered the MacDonald Clan living in Glencoe. I'll tell you about it when we're in the glen so that you can visualize it for yourself.

Right before Glencoe sits a place called the *Bridge of Orchy*: with a real bridge, an inn, and a railway station, all surrounded by gigantic mountains.

At the end of the trip, on the way to Glasgow airport, I have big plans to stop here for lunch, but now I hunger for what will be my fourth lifetime look at Glencoe. (Above: An artist rendition of Glencoe by Dorothy Bunny Bowen)

I remember the first time, thirty years back, in awe of the narrowness of glens squeezed by four thousand foot mountains on either side, thinking about the men, women and children, chassed down in a blizzard, bayonetted by red-coated British soldiers and dying of exposure in the snow.

As emerald green as Glencoe is, even in the sunlight it bodes dark and ghostly, because it is truly both, a haunted landscape.

I cannot imagine how the clans survived in these desolate Glens. But survive they did, on a diet centered around oats and meager livestock, and for ten centuries no less, living in isolation, in ignorance, but in an implicit state of liberty that one might envy.

Once in the glen itself, on a one-track road, I keep pointing out the original road meandering across the valley, sometimes to our right and sometimes to our left. The old road is still there, as are some of the stone "bridges" which carry it over the many streams coming down the steep mountains slopes.

But these graded dirt passageways were not there in 1692 when the massacre occurred; they were built during the "crofter" years, in the 1800's (more on the crofters later). Before these windy cart ways were built, the clan people used simple pathways that ran the length of the glen. Once off path – say to hunt deer in the upper mountains - one trudged in wet or frozen tundra, a mix of heathers, mosses, stones and the like.

Pulling over in the heart of the glen, I am ready to explain the massacre saga as I have come to see it:

In the early 1600's, England took control of Scotland by proclaiming dual kingdoms – that of England and that of Scotland ruled by a common King (James Stuart, described earlier) - but the highlanders did not buy into this obvious construct, remaining indignant. Later, King William of Orange, the protestant consolidator and replacement of the catholic Stuart line, proclaimed he would leave the clans to their primitive way of life so long as each clan chief signed an oath of loyalty to the new King, with a January 1, 1692 cut-off date.

On that date, all of the clans had delivered the pledge... but two: The MacDonalds of Glencoe had signed the paper, though delayed in delivering it on time due to the army representative being away from Fort William, off visiting Inverrary. MacIan, the MacDonald chief, wanting no trouble, rides down to Innverary in a blizzard and delivers the oath to the British officer on January 3rd.

The military brass reports back to the King, saying that all of the clans, but one, complied.

The King asks if other than the last holdout, were there any signs of resistance, and was told "no", though the MacDonalds were two days late due to the special trip through the snow.

The King, believing his January 1st edict absolute, and looking to show his resolve, orders a Scottish company of the King's army, to march into Glen Coe, to first befriend the MacDonald Clan – Scotsman to Scotsman - making them feel at ease, and then on a certain day, at a certain hour, to kill every man living in the glen, burn the houses, and leave the families destitute (Above, the troops and MacDonald's share a laugh).

After a week of being quartered in the clan huts up and down the valley, and after drinking many a nightly dram of whiskey with the clansmen, the signal was given, and in three different hamlets within the glen, the MacDonald men were shot and stabbed, as the woman and children ran for their lives into yet another blizzard, only to be hunted down by the alcohol-fueled soldiers, who bayonetted some of their innocent bodies, leaving others to freeze in the snow.

Before the King authorized the assassination order, he asked his secretary of state for comment. The secretary responded:

"That damnable sept (a branch of a Clan), the worst in the highlands. It would be a proper vindication of public justice to extirpate (remove by surgery) that sect of thieves."

As this was a military operation, the written orders from the king down remain even today. The final order given to the commanding officer in charge of the slaughter is as follows:

"You are hereby ordered to fall upon the rabelle, the MacDonalds of Glencoe, and put all to the sword under seventy. You are to have a special care that the old fox (Chief MacIan) and his sons doe not escape your hands. See that this be put in execution, without fear or favor, else you may expect to be dealt with as one not true to King and Country…"

This night has never been forgotten by the Highland Scotts, and in the end, it backfired on the King. Yes, the human race has inflicted worse atrocities as far as numbers of victims - Stalin, Hitler and Mao come to mind - but this evil came out of trust and intimacy between fellow Scotsmen, something uniquely disturbing. The Scots call it "murder under trust".

Once word spread throughout the Highlands, none held to the belief that British overlords could ever be appeased.

Every compromise would be exploited by London until the clans were fully marginalized. This mindset led to initial clan uprisings in the early 1700's, culminating in the final resistance at Culloden in 1746. Below, an excerpt from John Buchan's "Massacre At Glencoe"

"By five o'clock on the morning of Saturday 13th the wind had grown to a tempest and the snow was drifting heavily. Lieutenant Lindsey and a few soldiers presented themselves at Maclan's house and asked civilly to see the chief on a pressing matter. Maclan got out of bed shouting to bring the visitors a morning draught (of whiskey). Two shots were fired from behind, one in Maclan's back and one in his brain. Lady Glencoe was then stripped naked and the rings on her fingers removed by the soldier's teeth."

Fifty-three years later, in 1745, Chief Alasdair MacDonald of Glencoe led 125 of his men at Culloden, the last stand, and was subsequently captured and imprisoned.

1690 – Glen Coe Wilderness

1690 - the Queen Mary Stuart and her husband King William Of Orange, Monarchs of England, Wales Ireland & Scotland

Glencoe in 1931 – still desolate

Note: Lady Glencoe, whose rings were bitten off, escaped with hundreds of others over the mountains, but died during the journey of shock and exposure.

Glen Coe 2015 - Joseph/Cody and "The Beehive" stones.
The "old road", going across a stone bridge, sits in the background.

HIGHLANDERS - LOCH NESS

After Leaving the Glencoe valley, one meanders north to the town of Fort William, which sits right below Ben Nevis, which at 4,500 feet still wears August snow patches at its summit.

Fort William, as you might guess, was built by the English to stay close to the Highlanders – just in case. Above Fort William, Loch Ness presents itself.

But before continuing further north to Ness, there is the commitment, to stop at Inverlochy Castle for an afternoon tea.

Once, a real castle of that moniker stood on the shores of Loch Linnhe, but here I refer to a magnificent 5-star manor house sitting on the outskirts of Fort William, next to the aforementioned Inverlochy medieval ruins.

Just a word about Loch Linnhe... Linnhe is a saltwater loch that starts in Fort William, melding with the sea some 40 miles further south. It occupies an ancient geological depression called the Great Glen Fault. Further north, the fault holds Lock Ness, a fresh water body. This upper Ness section of the Great Glen "crevice" ends up at Inverness.

The *Great Glen Fault* cuts the west off from the rest of Scotland. The line from Fort William to Inverness is where Lock Ness sits; the open waterway below is Loch Linnhe.

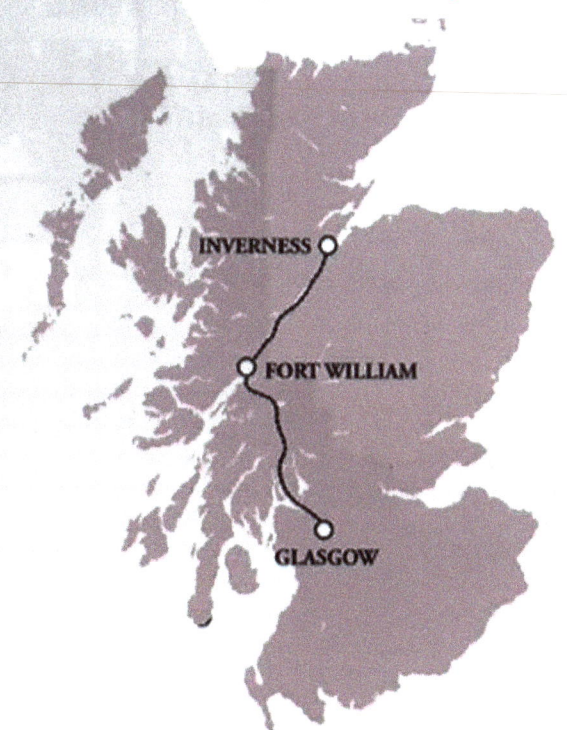

Islay, the furthest bit of land beyond Loch Linnhe proper, will be discussed later.

So finally, we pull up to Inverlochy Castle, for afternoon tea.

A most matron-looking woman stands at the front door; I role my window and inquire.

Is it too late for a tea?

Of course not, please come in.

I park the VW, and the family hops out, keen for a proper English tea – with scones, clotted cream, jellies, etc.

The older woman leads us into the house, hands us off to two younger women, who lead us to the grand living room. An August fire burns, and everything that can be good surrounds us.

Gratefully taking our places on the feathered couches and chairs, resting our bones from the long drive, feeling the fire, and having the whole place to ourselves, the house women appear thrilled by our arrival, assuring us that the tea service is…. Devine!

Off they go to fetch the royal particulars of an English tea. I wander over to the grand piano and sketch out a melody I had discovered back home, right before departure. Then I see them marching in with the trays.

Ah, here comes the feast, and I go back to the family all seated by the fire.

Teas, Coffees, Scones, Muffins, Shortbread and Sugar Cookies, Devonshire Clotted Cream, Butter and Jelly... all fit for a king. We dig in, thrilled to be able to experience the moment.

But our day's journey is not yet done. Up through Loch Ness, then Inverness and ultimately to Culloden House we must go, a few hours more. I pay the check, and amongst warm whishes from the house staff we depart.

(Below: Inverlochy Castle Hotel, and a patch of snow on Nevis)

On the road again.

Facing a few more hours of driving - on the wrong side of the road in a fairly large VW microbus - I take a deep breath, and think about what's coming next: Loch Ness, and a chance - if luck will have it - to see Nessie, the Loch Ness monster herself.

Ok, I admit it. Every time I drive along Lock Ness I look, just in case.

I will summarize the case for Nessie in a bit, but first let's look at the case against her existence.

Loch Ness Monster

Environment: As deep as the lock is, 900 feet, it is still a relatively small space when you think about other "fantasy" creatures, like *UFO aliens* who have the universe to call home, or *Bigfoot Apes*, who apparently dwell in forests everywhere on earth. Granted, there is no proof of these creatures any more than there is proof of Nessie, it's just that these larger environments make it more likely for creatures to survive and reproduce.

Numbers: Speaking of reproducing, there would need to be many Nessie monsters in the loch to create adequate genetic diversity to prevent inbreeding. If, say, 500 such creatures existed in the loch, one would spot them regularly.

Geography: Next, Lock Ness is 50 feet above sea level. Waters pour into the loch from the rain soaked mountain ranges that surround it, and water escapes – singularly - at the north end, through the Ness River, which slowly drops 50 feet as it finds its way to the sea at Inverness. Which begs the question: did the monsters swim upstream from the saltwater ocean to settle in the fresh water lake? And in any case, how do they breath?

History: As 4,000 years ago found the whole region covered in ice, the monsters could only have arrived in more recent years, and if so, there should be others somewhere else on earth. Similar legends come out of Lake Champlain, with a monster named "Champy". The Congo River houses a certain "Mokelembembe" and in a lake in British Columbia one can find "Ogopogo". But these too remain unsubstantiated.

Still, none of the objections prove absolute showstoppers; they just make Nessie improbable, which keeps the door, open.

According to The official *Loch Ness Monster Sightings Registry*, there have been over 1,000 recorded sightings, and many more left unrecorded.

The first documented sighting, noted in 565 AD by Saint Columba - the missionary who attempted to convert the Picts to Christianity - claims Columba came across some Picts rescuing a man from the monster. Columba invoked the name of Christ and sent the monster into a deep dive.

Many have led searches, including actor Charlie Sheen, who was out on a party boat for 48 hours without a sighting.

Formal searches, with submarines and sonar, led to nothing.

Plus there have been many admitted hoaxes causing confidence in Nessie to wane ... until you get there!

HIGHLANDERS - TORRIDON

The phrase "mind blowing" is sometimes used to describe extraordinary experiences that "leap frog" one's standard of what to expect on earth.

Well, if Scotland - overall - does not reach your "mind blowing" threshold, then certainly Torridon and its sister territory Applecross (covered in the next chapter) will.

The Torridons seen from the crest above Diabaig – on our way to lunch.

As the reader knows, I have traveled through these landscapes before, and have navigated their tiny roads, dwelling in numerous highland residences along the way. Still, now that I am again wandering Torridon and Applecross, I must say: it is good to be back, good to be humbled by the land itself!

Leaving *Culloden House* for *Torridon* we have two choices: a direct, two-hour southern journey over the dual-cart-way A832 to Kinlochewe, where the "expressway" shrinks down to the A896, a single-tract road weaving through the Torridon Mountains ... or

An eight-hour coastal journey traversing towards *Ullapool*, passing the *An Tealleach* mountain range, then bending around to the "big" town of *Gairloch*, all on a single-track road. At Gairloch we are nowhere near our destination.

Beyond Gairloch, the mentioned coast road turns inland, back towards Kinlochewe, where it meets up with that same single-tract road (the A896) described earlier, winding the Torridon Mountain Valley.

I pick the long way; I had driven it before, knowing it worth the travel pain. So we venture forth, heading to the coast, our driver, (myself) soon recalling that one-tract roads twist and buckle with every expression of the terrain; sometimes the road demands driving at five miles per hour just to avoid one's own death and destruction.

Once committed to the long loop road circling the province of *Wester Ross* – and please note: there are no other roads in *Wester Ross* – reality sets in.

The mountain ranges of Wester Ross

Accepting the gravity of my decision, I immediately adopt a French philosophy called *je ne regrettes rein*, AKA "no regrets". I drive on stoically. More amazingly, no one within the family circle complains of the decision, though the question "how much longer" does come up, usually at moments where I wonder the very same point.

The Dundonnell WW II memorial, with various clan surnames listed

Along this longer route, I yearn for two milestones to confirm our progress:

Dundonnell, a hamlet at the foot of *An Teallach Mountain,* and *Gairloch,* the "beach" town along the coast.

An Teallach stands a prized mountain for climbers, and years ago, before children, Laura and I stopped the car and climbed partway up, never reaching the summit's April snowfields. Still, An Teallach (below) stays forever in my mind.

Continuing onwards, one finally drives forever along the coast, spotting many sandy coves and beaches, warmed by the Gulf Stream.

    A favorite stop is *Inverewe Gardens*, built in a protected cove by an eccentric gardener, housing all kinds of exotic plants and trees, including palm trees, able to survive due to the cove's Gulf Stream warmth. This is as north as Hudson Bay, Canada.

    Finally we reach *Gairloch,* an enclave with a beach, a golf course, and numerous accommodations. I have always sensed that I resided here a Jacobite in another life.

    Once in April, Laura and I settled into Gairloch for a few nights... the sun shining, spring lambs filling the fields, peat fires burning in the village cottages. We were young, elated. But upon checking in at a local inn, we found a kilted proprietor in different spirits. I remember him saying:

    Lad, yes the sun shines today, but we locals have not begun to recover. Ye must know that each winter it just rains and rains night and day - for six straight months mind you!

    Ya see, we're still just a bit ragged.

    These collective memories of Gairloch inspired a particular lyric in my *Scotland* song as follows:

Well the rain has ended, spring lambs climb them hills; the peat fires are burning; do you love me still?

As we were behind schedule, needing to reach *Torridon House* in time for dinner, I simply stopped at the Gairloch petrol station, filled the tank, breathed the salt air, revisited memories, and then got back in the van, bracing myself for the drive into the Torridon Mountain Range.

From Gairloch, the road next follows a long stretch, along the shore of Loch Maree. The surrounding mountain rock formations soon become pink in color, the trademark of the Torridon range.

Up on a high mountain ridge we spot a buck deer holding court, staring down on us. Other than the single-track road and us, there is no sign of humanity – no cars, houses, electric poles, etc., just mountains, native pines, water and sky.

The Loch Maree road is quite elegant, though invoking one's image of another planet. But once reaching the tiny village of Kilochewe, one enters the heart of the Torridon's, a vibe definitively forbidding in demeanor (see below).

At least we are closing in on our destination - *Torridon House*. It is just down the valley, situated where the valley floor ends and *Loch Torridon*, a sea extension of the valley begins framed by the same Torridon range for another twelve miles, until reaching the open sea (*above*).

Finally we arrive, and there it sits on the shore of the loch – *Torridon House*.

Sometime in the mid-1800's, a wealthy man began construction on this property. All materials were boated in from distant suppliers, and it took 30 years to finish the house.

Fourteen years ago in 2001, when we last stayed at *Torridon House*, new proprietors had just started their run of the place. Our own son Joseph was then almost two years of age. On this 2015 visit, as we pull up, a young man of sixteen greets us, and after I dig a bit, find him to be the son of the proprietors I had meet years ago. Now he, and my son are the same age, both strapping, handsome sixteen-year olds, each with a destiny.

Up to our rooms: to rest, to bathe in hot bathtubs, and to dress for dinner. The family agrees to meet for drinks at 7:30 downstairs in the living room parlor.

I could not wait to sample the whisky collection. Like Culloden House, Torridon boasts an extensive whisky selection, and I put the young connoisseur running the bar in charge of picking two for me before dinner.

While having our drinks, a woman from the dining room greets us, handing out the evening menus, plus the wine list to peruse. A few minutes later she takes our order. We sit back on the living room couches, finish our drinks, and a bit later she reappears saying our table has been readied. Entering the dining room, my wine selections await on the table; we sit, and instantly the hot bread and soup appear, as the sommelier pours the first round of white wine.

Torridon House Whiskey Bar

The next day is hiking day. Driving back on the road we came in on, we spot a trail head, park, and get out to read the sign before proceeding. One is warned: if one climbs to the top and begins to follow the trail across the high 3,000-foot ridge, that there is no intermediate escape off of the ridge. The trail is 8 miles long, and the entry/exit points sit on either end.

Secondly, the sign explains that fencing has been run in many places to keep the deer at bay, hoping that trees will grow. This was the most ridiculous thing I had heard of in some time; I sensed a government "make work" project.

As far as the actual climb, we didn't get far by professional standards, though made it above the heather line into the sheer rock level. We all passed on negotiating the 8 miles of ridge terrain, 3-4 thousand feet up (photos follow).

Back down the mountain by hour two, we all agree to find lunch – "find" being the correct optic. Being research oriented (meaning Google), I describe a "find" to my grateful family: *Gille Brighde*, a remote café only 9 miles away!

The Gille Brighde web site describes what to expect: ...*destination Diabaig, on the shore of Loch Torridon - enjoy the journey and let us take care of your rest. It is a special place, and whether by sea or by road we think the destination is definitely worth the journey!*

I wonder what they are talking about?

I described our dining option to all, and all agree; we will get into the VW micro-bus and drive the far side of Loch Torridon – opposite Torridon House – along an impossible road to have lunch in a place called Lower Diabaig.

The bottom line: after all I had experienced in Scotland for decades, I am shocked at the ridiculous, impossible road I next survive, and the audacity of these far-fetched restaurant owners to trick people into finding them. Later, I realize, it was the best lunch excursion ever!

After all, I am alive to write about it!

Not that we were ever close to death; it just felt like that. Thankfully our VW microbus had automatic transmission; otherwise I may have expired of "cortisol hormonal overdose" while frozen on a very bad pin-turn, straddling a cliff.

Finally descending from the mountain pass, we spy the tiny village down below on the Loch Torridon bank.

As we descend further we pass various long-abandoned crofter stone homes in what once must have been "Upper Diabaig".

Once at the very bottom I take a breath, drive past the restaurant, and park the van next to a great pier that is more formidable than the whole village.

Stepping into the restaurant, our host, a big burley fellow who seems gentle, though looks like a pirate, greets us warmly. A group of five is just leaving so we take their table, as I nod to an older couple sitting behind me. I did not want to sit, so I walk back to the bar, and my pirate host pours me a double Highland Whiskey, getting beers out for the rest of the family.

I found your web site, I started to tell him, *but it never mentioned the road.*

I know, but at least I warn people that it's worth the journey.

Why here?

Me wife – that's her do'in the cook'n – and I did restaurant jobs all over and decided to go out on our own. The village said the schoolhouse was available, so I took it – 'bout two years ago.

So this was a schoolhouse?

In operation for 50 years. Kids on the other side of the pass walked here everyday. Then the old families disappeared and those here today don't have children, so there you have it.

But the road is frightening. How do you get supplies in, and from where?

Ah that! There's these little businesses that bring ya what you need. Place an order on Monday and on Tuesday they go to Inverness or Fort William, pick up the stuff and on Wednesday they drive around dropping it all off.

While chatting, as my host keeps busy, through the window, I notice a couple drive up on bicycles. I step outside to greet them.

Pointing up: Did you just come in over that road?

We had no idea what it was like, and just kept coming. Now we made it.

But you need to get back.

How's the food?

Haven't had it yet but everything looks great.

Back inside I go over to my table and tell everyone that the couple about to come in actually rode their bikes here. Everyone cringes. I address this to the older couple sitting behind me as well. They look keen for a chat, so I turn my chair sideways to fit them in.

They had driven down from Sutherland up north, a hundred miles away. *Came here to get away from people.*

Two redheads in their 70's, with quick eyes and pleasant dispositions, he sporting very long hair tied in a pony tale as well as an 18 inch beard also tied in a pony tale: quite a look.

They reveal that they are old school conservatives, detesting socialism, and they go on to tell me about their views. Then comes the lunch, which I quickly dispose of. I excuse myself, to sit in the VW, smoke a cigar and stare across the loch.

Stepping outside the schoolhouse, though, another bunch of people approach, and I ask;

How did you get here?

By boat: tied up on the other side.

Well I drove, and there's two in there that bicycled in; you guys did it right.

Smoking my cigar, the family comes out and wanders down the beach to investigate a wrecked ship and start skimming stones.

My pony-tailed friend comes over to chat some more, but I see two new figures walking towards us, this time with walking poles.

Hold on, I've got to find out if they actually walked here.

Getting out of the van I intersect the poor young souls.

Did you walk here?

Yes along the edge of the loch, but it was all rocks and very wet.

How long did that take?

Five hours.

Five hours – geeze! And next you'll be taking the road back I hope.

Definitely.

Well I can give you a lift. Think about it and I'll check inside before I go.

My ponytail friend and I watch the walkers disappear into the schoolhouse and he comments:

The Proprietors

A steady stream of us wanderers parade through here all day long. Even at the end of the earth they (the restaurant owners) make a go of it, and I say, 'Well good for them'.

Footnote: The walkers turned the ride down; we drove back to Torridon House

Settling in for another evening of drinks and dinner, a quick storm passes, blessing all with a glorious rainbow.

As the sun sets, the streetlights of the tiny village of Torridon, across the way, come on. They are quite proud of these lights.

Ok, tomorrow off to Applecross. Wild flowers on the Torridon mountainside

Joseph in the Torridon House living room before dinner.

Laura on a Torridon hill top.

Part – III – The Sea

Applecross, Crofters & The Clearings

I have only visited *Applecross* in the spring and summer months, and wonder how the few people who live here get by the rest of the year.

Taking a sharp right off the main road at Shieldaig, we follow a single-track coastal road that circles around towards Applecross hamlet, our lunchtime destination.

Note: The road to Lower Diabaig, yesterday's lunch place, is shown on the far side of Loch Torridon.

After lunch we will exit Applecross town by navigating the treacherous *Pass Of The Cattle*, an old drovers trail, where annually, local crofters transported their steeds to inland railheads, which brought the "goods" down to Glasgow.

The image of Applecross Crofter men driving cattle over mountains stays with me. Following Culloden in 1746, it is hard to picture that these once independent clansmen ended as crofters: indentured servants, slaves even, with their highland valleys turned into sheep farms by their own Clan Chieftain Lairds.

Note: "Croft" is an old Anglo-Saxon word for field and Lairds is a Scottish word for Lords.

The clearings systematically replaced the clan system with the crofter system. Rather than the chief dolling out land to clan families to till their food and tend their cattle, *the Lairds* went into business with the English, turning their properties into vast wool producing concerns.

The wool from this "mass-production sheep factory" found its way down to the English industrial cities for textile production. Anyone not working on sheep and wool was left without a source of income, hence many willingly got on boats for America and other places of refuge. Those staying behind to work the field became Crofters, hired hands, no longer a clansman.

Crofter hut ruins

Over time, as the former chiefs began to reap great profits in the wool trade, many left the highlands to move into townhouses in Edinburg, Glasgow and London.

Where previously the little clansman could count on the clan chief's fairness, the helpless crofter family survived at the mercy of these absentee landlords, who allocated land parcels and huts to them, one year at a time. During this one-year posting, crofters were assigned to clear nearby sections of the Laird's land in preparation for introducing sheep the following year.

The next season found the crofter family relocated somewhere else on the estate, with a new croft to garden, a new stone hut to live in, and another section of the estate to get ready for even more sheep.

Huts in the 1800's

One of the many sheep roaming free along the Applecross one-track road.

The resulting reduction in the Scottish population from 4 million to 2 million was accompanied by another change, the expansion of Glasgow and Edinburg; if not shipped off to America, many of the remaining Scotts ended up in one of these two cities which became ship building and agricultural distribution centers during the industrial revolution.

This left very few people living on the land, and those that remained in rural settings owed their complete existence to the Lairds.

Today, land ownership is still concentrated, with vast Scottish estates owned by a few hundred landowners – many of them from outside of the United Kingdom. Most of the little white houses one sees are crofter rental arrangements.

Remnants of old crofter huts are scattered along the shore of Applecross. The section of road seen above, runs south towards Applecross village. Two crofter huts have been given modern roofs. I don't know their current function, possibly people still live in them.

Note: across the water lies one of the outer islands sitting between the Applecross peninsula and the big island of *Skye*. These outer islands are filled with birds and seals, reached by sea kayaks one can rent in Applecross.

As seen, the coastal area spreads out nicely below the road, and an unfenced mountainous terrain climbs sharply above, where tagged sheep roam free until sheered. In crofter terms, the upper rugged land is communal, called an *outfield*, with fenced in land closer to the crofter house called an *infield*.

Applecross, the main village, has 5 or 6 smaller satellite enclaves on the peninsular, each dotted with a few white houses built next to old crofter huts. I cannot imagine what these isolated residents, these modern crofters, live off of. In the old crofter days of Applecross, Highland Cattle, a unique breed, grazed on this bottomland, but the herds are long gone.

Getting all of this beef to market led to the annual droving exercise, which entailed a 2,000-foot climb over the *Pass Of The Cattle* (photos coming up shortly). Below, we spied a bull, from another breed of cattle. This guy was fenced in.

As we drove through this terrain, past the little hamlets, I kept an eye out for the old walking trail, the one used for hundreds of years before the one-track road we now drove on arrived in the 1960's. The old trail linked the hamlets together, and we could spot it here and there.

During the potato famine of 1850 – the same famine that struck Ireland where the Irish landlords (Enlishmen) allowed tenants to starve to death – I read that the *Laird of Gairloch* (an actual Scott) opened up his pocket book – just a bit.

To put money into the purses of local desperate crofters, the Laird paid them to build a proper grass road, with little stone bridges that cut through the moorland. *A remnant below:*

The old walking path

Finally, civilization, Applecross itself, seen across the cove as we round a bend; it consists of few buildings, with *The Applecross Inn* our target for lunch. As we drive around the cove we first pass the *Clachan Church*, self-described as follows:

Standing on the ancient site of St Maelrubha's church (673 AD), the present church was built in 1817. The beauty and tranquillity of the surroundings complement the quiet simplicity of the plain stone building. To the left of the gate stands a tall, plain slab with an incised Celtic cross, said to mark the grave of Ruairidh Mor MacAogan, abbot of Applecross, who died in 801 AD. The remains of carved Celtic crosses, dating from the 8th century, are in glass cases in the heritage centre opposite. The church is recommended for its simplicity and peace, a fitting heritor of the old Gaelic name of 'A Chomraich' - the Sanctuary.

Applecross is hopping; it's Saturday and bikers willing to navigate the *Pass Of The Cattle* are coming and going, grabbing food, beers and whiskeys from the *Applecross Inn* pub.

I am pumped, hungry, and ready to be part of the action. The pub is packed.

The pup owner spots my family of six coming through the door, with a bunch of bikers right behind us. I glance at the twenty or so tables in view not finding an empty chair. The proprietor waves to one of the waitresses; she opens a door to an empty dining room with five additional tables. We sit; I next go to the bar, returning a few minutes later to find all five tables filled.

The whole family has beer to start; I let my fetched glass of whiskey sit for now and quench my thirst like the others with a pint of beer, greatly needed after the long ride in.

Good, hearty comfort food, and now we grab our beers to hang out street-side, taking in the biker action, resting for what is yet to come.

Skimming rocks across from the Applecross Inn, Cody, Laura and Joseph

Joseph wondering why movie directors don't come here and film scenes from other planets.

At the summit, note the roads only guardrail; why just here?

Cody and the VW, the "engine that could"

What was next was The Pass Of The Cattle, below!

Goodbye Applecross

Exiting the Pass Of The Cattle heading to Kyle Of Lochalsh and then to Skye, both many hours away.

SKYE, ISLAY, WHISKY & CLAN DONALD

Skye from our single engine seaplane

A previous chapter described the *Glen Coe* MacDonald's and mentioned *Somerled*, the original MacDonald patriarch, the first *Lord Of The Isles*, whose descendants ruled the islands for 300 years before accepting Scottish King overlords around 1490, and not going down quietly – a troublesome lot.

Castle ruins on Skye

And so, reconsider Glen Coe, years later in the winter of 1692, when the English King William orders the massacre of the Glen Coe MacDonald's - not for the MacDonald's arriving late with their pledge, but solely due to them being MacDonald's, people used to doing their own thing for six centuries. In executing local MacDonald's, the King proclaims *absolute monarchy* to all, a special broadcast to the Scotch Irish highlanders, and a specific broadcast to the MacDonald chieften then residing in *Duntulm Castle* on the *Isle of Skye*

Note: It is thought that the vikings named it *Skye* as the mountains came out of the ocean to touch the clouds.

In 1490, when the MacDonalds lost their sea kingdom to the Scottish King, their headquarters then sat on *Islay*, 50 miles south of *Skye*. But in 1490, when Clan Donald fell, the Scottish King gave Islay over to the *Campbells*, a rival clan. This set back will be described later in the chapter.

The 1490 *MacDonalds*, though, forced out of Islay, still had castles up in Skye, and were allowed to make Skye home. And with these introductory things said, let's look into the overall MacDonald saga, covering *Skye, Islay, Whiskey* and of course, the *MacDonalds*.

On previous visits to Scotland I never made it to Skye, though once staying overnight in Kyle of Localsh, where the Skye ferry once ran.

Now, in 2015, signs for "the bridge" appear, and an impressive span of engineering soon radiates rather than a ferry.

But before crossing, we stop at the *Localsh Hotel* for a tea, where I once stayed for but that one night many years ago. We have coffee and tea, and then, off to Sky via the bridge.

Once over the bridge, as Skye has only one main road, we start down it, eventually taking a left to *Sleat* and *Kinloch Lodge*, our new home for three nights.

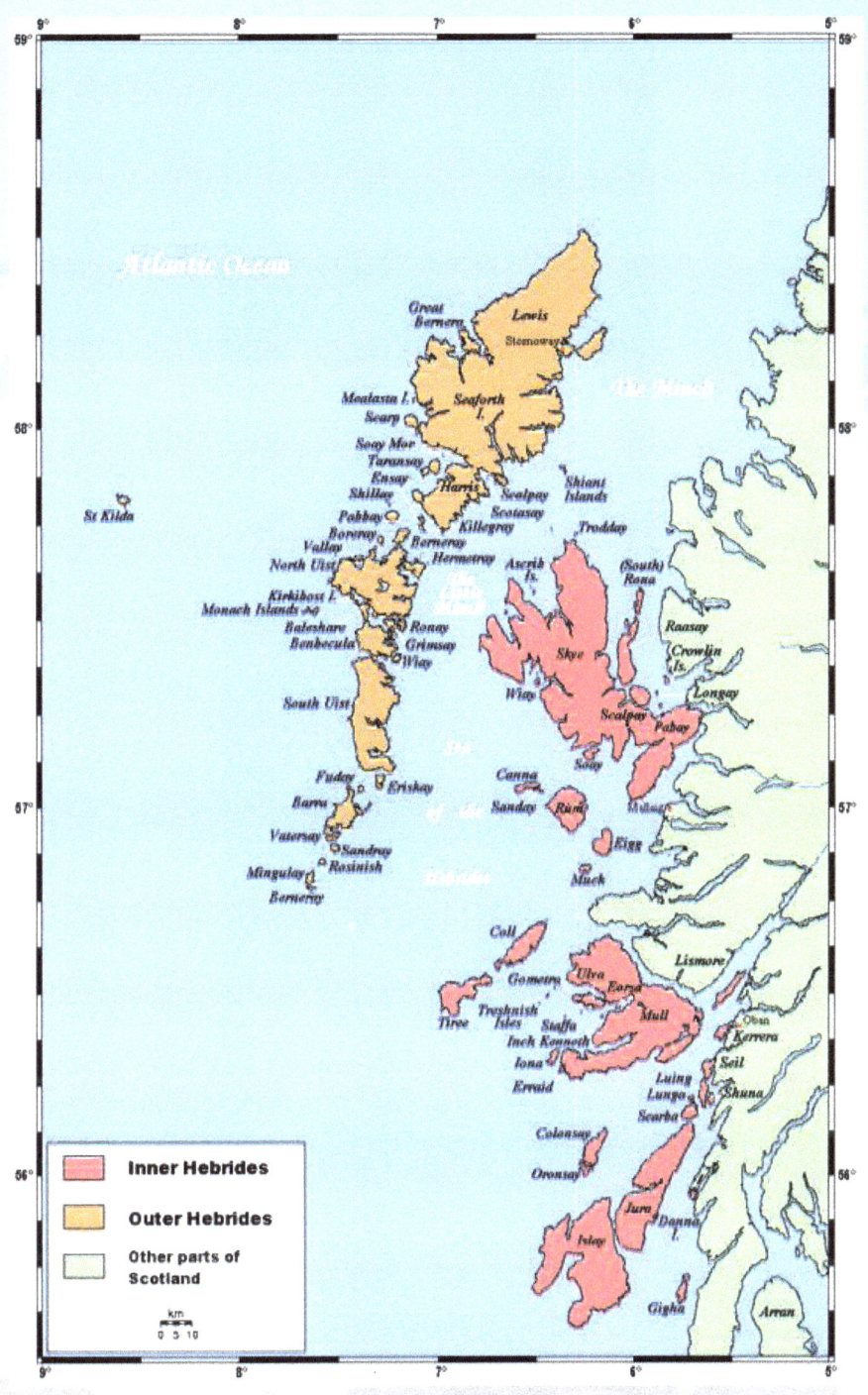

The Island Kingdom

Skye, one might notice, sits in the center of the island realm, with Islay quite south of it.

Notice also, the already mentioned *St Kilda* way out past the *Lewis & Harris* chain.

"Clan Donald famed for galleys and tall swift ships"

When Somerled, the MacDonald patriarch (who died 1164) assembled his island kingdom - previously under Viking control for a hundred and fifty years – Somerled was certainly the phenomenon of his time.

Figurine of Somerled

His mother a descendent of the Norwegian King "Magnus Barefoot", and Somerled's father, a sixth generation Scotch Irish Gillebrede from Ireland, made quite a pair.

Accordingly, the offspring boy Somerled, probably stayed ambivalent regarding his racial lines; in adulthood, Somerled simply wanted a kingdom, and to get one, he needed to defeat the Norse lords then in power aligned to Norway.

And so, somehow Somerled, a warrior chief of unimaginable abilities, one that only comes along every few centuries, systematically conquers innumerable Norse lords, island by island, making them all pledge fidelity to Somerled and not to Oslo, Norway.

Somerled in old Gaelic

There are accounts of Somerled attacking with 50, and 100 longboats of the Norse style, from the Isle of Man northward, subduing those in power. Decades later, Somerled never stopped his conquering ways, finally dying in battle on the mainland, taking on another Celtic Chief, Malcolm of Argyle, who nobly, they say, sent Somerled's body back to Somerled's surviving sons for burial.

A MacDonald coin, featuring the long ship.

I am only giving the reader a glimpse of life back then.

One might find this interesting. The original MacDonald Gaelic name is MacDhomhnuill, which means "sons (Mac) of the world ruler". The MacDonald motto: *By sea and by land.*

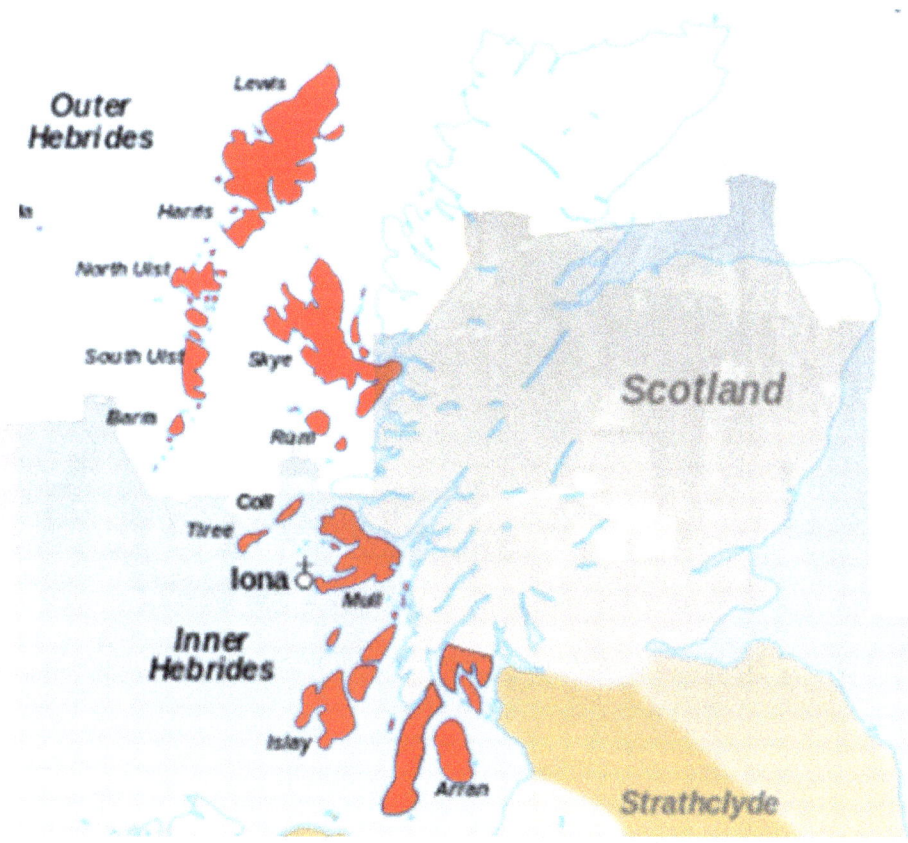

No kidding!

The reader might wonder how I uncover these things, and the answer: I go to the places involved, letting locals teach me memories.

With this said, the topic of *Islay*, the aforementioned island below Loch Linne, and the first seat of the MacDonald's, can be brought forward.

I explored Islay eighteen years ago in 1997, when my young family, sister and brother-in-law visited its distilleries and the ruins of the MacDonald stronghold, *Finlaggan Castle*. It was mind blowing!

Based upon my experience back then, tourists don't go to Islay. We were it, staying at a terrific inn that maintains a seaside links golf course, with world famous Whiskey distilleries all around, the graves of early MacDonald's nearby. For my brother-in-law Ken and myself it was heaven, because as you will see: we were on a mission from God.

Above, the distilleries of Islay

In 1997 I resided in New York City, and had an office in London as well, with both locations providing access to the finest, rare Scotch Whiskies available anywhere on earth.

Above, the distilleries of Islay, the seat of whiskey.

Over time I experienced many a fine bottle with brother-in-law Ken (a Scotch MacKenzie), and other imbibers, including my father-in-law Phil (a pure Scott 'Britain', as in Briton).

We become fond of the eleven Islay whiskey distilleries, learning Islay to be the very place where monks invented whiskey back in the 1400's. I guess plenty of peat, water, and a reliable supply of barley does the trick, along with monks with enough time on their hands to spark the discovery.

Well, after years of drinking Islay whiskies, I encounter a special bottle at Sherry Lehman, a high-end retailer in NYC, labeled: *Society of Malt Drinkers, 1971, Islay.*

The label lists the barrel number and the date, but not the distillery! Oh well who cares if it is as good as it looks.

Back home we try it. A simple drop floats on one's tongue, and when swallowed, the warmest, deepest ripple of goodness echoes through the whole body: nothing like it on earth. Repeatedly we taste the tiniest droplets imaginable to re-experience the effect over and over, doubting that what we felt was real.

Finishing that bottle, I buy another, then another, then another, finely stopping into Sherry Lehman one day to find that there are no more bottles – and that meant no more bottles anywhere: whatever keg the whiskey came from, the bottles sold out, full stop, go home.

I stood shocked.

Our last bottle still held two inches of the stuff, and suddenly realizing the preciousness of the remaining stash, Ken and I decide not to drink it, instead choose to go to Islay, find the distillery behind the batch, hoping to purchase more should more exist. It takes a few years, but finally we head over to Scotland – with the bottle - landing at Glasgow's Paisley airport, switching to a smaller plane that carries us to Islay.

Very jet lagged, upon checking into the inn, Ken and I play a round of golf on the Inn's empty, magnificent links course, and afterwards bull our way forward, driving over to the *Ardbeg* distillery, to start the quest for God's kindness – the greatest whisky ever made.

Arriving at *Ardbeg Distillery*, Ken, myself, and my older daughter Cody find the master distiller who manages both *Ardbeg* and nearby *Laphroaig*. We show him the bottle and proclaim its value to the human race. He, in his sixties, a life long Islay resident, having made whisky for forty years at most of the islands distilleries, ignores our bottle, saying: *Lads there have been many a fine whiskeys made over the years, let me show you how it's done.*

With this he gives us a thorough tour of the facility, explaining that now a days, with Ardbeg and most of the others owned by companies like Seagrams, everything is automated, so that every batch and every barrel comes out the same.

In the old days - back when our special bottle was created - each batch of peat water and barley was cooked somewhat randomly, and the barrels that cured the whiskeys ran the gamut, all of them from the United States, having cured American Bourbon first, then re-used here to cure Scotch Whiskey, with different barrels affecting the Scotch based upon how much Bourbon had seeped into the barrel's wood while in America.

Islay itself faces the sea, with sea storms carrying bits of salt water gleaned from the ocean onto the island throughout the year. This salt-tinged rainwater seeps down through forty feet of peat, and trickles out in little steams back to the ocean. Each distillery sits by one of these streams, using its salted, peated water as the base for the whiskey.

With all of these variables – the waters, the batch cooking combinations and the barrel effects – every once in a while a miracle barrel presents itself, selling better than gold to London merchants and whiskey buying clubs. But from what the master just said, it seems that conditions for miracle barrels are disappearing fast across all of Scotland.

With that, the master takes us to his tasting room to show off what he means, pouring three top-flight whiskeys into our little whiskey glasses, all the while ignoring our special bottle sitting on the table. Twenty minutes later…

Ready to try our bottle? I inquire.

Sure lad, let's give it a try.

I pour each of us a dram. It has been two years since last experiencing the magic, and suddenly I doubt myself. Maybe we exaggerated our bottle, a fantasy.

We three take our first drop; immediately our bodies reverberate from its profound potency, expanding its effect as it makes its way down the pipe to the stomach and beyond. It is surreal. The master suddenly explodes, crying (actually):

LADS, LADS, THIS IS THE FINEST HOOCH I HAVE EVER LAID ME HANDS ON!

He quickly identifies it as a *Bruichladdich* (an Islay distillery), saying he worked Bruichladdich in 1971 when the bottle was made.

Hmm…

We three drink the dram slowly, staring at each other in wonder after each small sip, with the jet lag Ken and I arrived with long gone.

A moment after the cups empty, the master looks down at the bottle, still with enough hooch for a second pour, and he gives us a look.

I know Ken wants to bring it back to America, and so do I, as this remaining inch is it for all time, but I become sentimental and proclaim: *We brought it here, and here it stays!* And so we pour and drink the last drops of the greatest hooch ever made by God through the hands of mankind.

Now as much as this 1997 adventure taught about whiskey, I would learn one more lesson about "unfiltered whiskey" while on Skye, eighteen years later, during this most recent 2015 trip. I will cover this latest whisky insight once the chapter turns back to Skye, but we are not yet finished with Islay.

Ruins of Finlaggan Castle, seat of the MacDonalds

The next day, traversing the empty island of Islay, we spy the various distilleries dotting the land as we work our way to the far extremities of the island, where the ruins of *Finlaggan Castle* sit, the original seat of the Lords Of The Isles.

So secure were the MacDonald's in this their strong hold that *Finlaggan Castle* had no walls, just a small bit of land with MacDonald residences and servant quarters, surrounded by water. The long boats came and went daily, bringing news and issue from each of the kingdom's many islands, returning with decrees from the Chief. This ruling method lasted for many, many generations.

Wandering around the castle ruins we find the burial ground for some of the MacDonald Chiefs.

Now lets get back to the story of how the MacDonald lost Islay, retreating up to Skye:

In 1427 the Scottish King, James I, in league with the Stewarts, trick the MacDonald's and other rivals into attending a "Parliament" in Inverness. James blindsides his enemies sending them to the dungeon. In retaliation, MacDonald's burn Inverness to the ground. Eventually, though, the MacDonald's are worn down and in 1492 join the Scottish Kingdom as vassals, meaning they can keep their land and castles - but not *Islay*, that prize goes to the Campbell's. The MacDonald's sail north to Skye, meeting kin residing on Skye.

But the forfeiture of the island kingdom let other clans, previously under the thumb of the MacDonald's, to also establish themselves as independent vassals of this absentee Scottish King seated so far away in Stirling. Without the MacDonald's, the Highland Scotch/Irrish chiefs operate freely again, as is their nature, and are soon hated by both The Scottish Lowland and English Kings. *"Suche wild savages voide of God's feare and our obedience"*

One such clan, Clan Macleod, "hold fast", lived on the western side of Skye, separated from the MacDonald's by the Cullin Mountains.

The MacLeod distillery, *Talikster*, one should note, still goes strong today. MacLeod kinfolk also resided further out in the Harris Islands.

Around 1600, the two Skye clans feud often, and the MacLeod Chief finally goes to MacDonald with a peace offering. MacLeod will give his sister to MacDonald, and following the practice of the day; the sister stays with MacDonald for a year. If she produces a male heir, then they marry, creating a blood bond between the two clans. If no male heir results, MacLeod takes his sister back.

No male heir comes of the co-habitation; instead during the year the sister goes blind in one eye. MacDonald is so disgusted with the outcome, that he blinds both a horse and a dog in one eye, ties the sister facing backwards on the blinded horse, and has the blinded dog, horse and backward sister led to the MacLeod Castle.

The MacLeod's go nuts. Relatives from Harris are called in and the whole lot of them descends upon the MacDonald's.

Hundreds die until the two chiefs decide adequate blood has been spilled to offset the perceived insults. Truce declared - the survivors sit together drinking vast quantities of whiskey.

Or so the story goes...

The MacDonald's of Skye show up again during the "45"...

This time, as Bonnie Prince Charlie escapes from Culloden and for five long months works his way across the highlands, eventually skulking off to Skye... there he "befriends" Flora MacDonald, then twenty-two years of age, who takes charge of Charlie's ultimate escape. Above: *David Niven as Charlie*.

Flora dresses Charlie as a woman, so that no one can track him, and gets Charlie onto a French frigate, returning him safely back to Paris for Charlie's aforementioned life of debauchery.

Ok, so now it is 2015, one thousand years since Somerled carved out his island kingdom, and five hundred years since the MacDonald's moved from Islay to Skye, and now we are on Skye. Let's charter a seaplane and look around.

Days before renting a plane, though, we check into *Kinloch House*, situated in the *Sleat* district of *Skye*, a beautiful property near the water's edge, facing a wide, protected salt water straight, looking out at mainland Scotland in the distance, and sure enough... more MacDonald stuff surfaces.

Kinloch House is owned by the seventeenth generation MacDonald's, direct descendants of Somerled, and this, as you might imagine, helped me choose Kinloch House for our three nights in Skye, but the fact that the house featured a Michelin starred chef mattered just as much.

That's Isabella MacDonald and Chef Marcello Tully in the photo. I never meet Marcello, but Isabella is a great hostess, fun to chat with and in doing so, she finds pointers to bolster one's visit. And, the MacDonald's have a good whiskey bar as well, which can't hurt in that part of the world.

Kinloch steps leading to water edge

Jolene at Kinloch House

I just realized: after all of the historical detail conveyed so far in this chapter, the reader may have lost track of our day: we left Torridon in the morning, had lunch in Applecross, tea at Kyle Of Localsh before crossing the Skye Bridge, finally arriving Kinloch House at 7 PM.

We set dinner for 8:30 PM, but before heading for our rooms, we are served Champaign and canapés in the living room, just to take the edge off.

Laura and Joseph look across to the mainland

At waters edge, Cody senses insects

The next morning a hike is decreed by the family, traversing another old drovers trail, this one cut across the hills above the house, reaching a thousand year remnant of a Norse settlement.

The old drovers trail

Unlike other branches of MacDonald's, like the Glen Coe bunch, *The MacDonald's of Sleat*, did not show up at Culloden in 1746, and were allowed to hold onto their property thereafter.

By the 1800's, the Sleat MacDonald's had mellowed, becoming proper *Lairds*, collecting rents from those tending their sheep and cattle. MacDonald livestock walked along this drover path to where the

Skye Bridge now stands; they were then ferried across to Kyle Of Localsh where the railhead sits, to be carted off to Glasgow, along with the Applecross cattle.

Cody covers up from midges bugs

Old MacDonald castle entrance

After the hike, our appetites up, we head off to the main event, a fifteen-minute drive to the MacDonald Castle built in the 1800's, now a ruin, but fronted by an excellent museum and sandwich shop. Here I would get the skinny on Somerled, plus they have instructors to teach how to throw battleaxes – a perfect afternoon.

Laura/Joe on the castle grounds

The museum is top of the line, presenting the whole arc of the Scotch Irish from 500 onward, the mainline story staying with Clan Donald for the last 950 years. I learn Somerled's mother to be Norse, descended from the Oslo King, and discover the expanse of an island empire held together by hundreds of swift-sailing long boats, with exchanges between islands taking place every a day or two.

After absorbing what I can, I speak to the curator about Somerled's Norse and Irish heritage and my ideas for a Scotland book.

The curator soon invites me to use their library, as a few weeks spent in the library would allow me to uncover countless, telling incidents of past lives; but alas, my living family waits outside, ready for the axe throwing segment of the afternoon.

Battle Axe Training

On the way back to the hotel, Laura points out a tiny sign with "Whisky" and an arrow on it, pointing to a small lane running down to the water. Hey, why not... I turn off.

The lane soon finds a small hamlet nestled by the water, with a shop selling fine woolens and I spy another sign with "whiskey" pointing to a house 'round back.

Stepping inside, I find a young woman and a display of just four whiskey bottles branded *Gaelic Whiskey*.

What is Gaelic Whisky? I inquire.

It is unfiltered whiskey; the way whiskey was made for centuries before modern times.

Tell me more.

Well, in the past three decades, the big spirit companies wanted a whiskey for the American market that would not get foggy when water or ice is mixed in, and they found that filtering the whiskey coming out of the barrels achieves this.

But, I interrupt, *that means that the physical traces of the barley, peat and wood are removed.*

Exactly, she affirms, *which affects both the body and flavor of the spirit. Drinking filtered whiskey is like drinking colored water, with just a hint of the foundation materials tasted.*

I bought four bottles, figuring I could get more in the states, as she said Gaelic Whiskey has American importers.

Back home, I realize the difference. One can really drink unfiltered whiskey on a continuum basis, due to its weight, and you will have to use will power to stop drinking it, rather than feeling you've had enough.

Back at Kinloch House, and another fine dinner bookended by more flights of whiskey, we settle down for our second night on Skye: tomorrow, the seaplane.

Joe and the pilot, his new BFF, both born in 1952

Jolene & Joseph

Cody & Laura

Skye From the Sea Plane

The Mallaig Ferry

HOMEWARD BOUND

Truth be told, I hesitate to write this last segment of the book, as it will certainly embody the last engraved thoughts I might ever notate on Scotland.

Our way home is a long one – starting from Skye, an outer Scottish Island, traversing through Glasgow, then through both London and New York - to finely reach our rural abode in northern Connecticut.

From *Skye*, we travel by ferry to *Mallaig* a town set across from Skye, over on the mainland. We next drive forever through the *Argyle* region, seeing – thank God – for a second time in my life,

The Five Sisters of Kincaid, a configuration of emerald mountains, clustered together, engulfing many trapped inland lakes, this entire geological configuration hugged by winding roads that simply wear you out.

MacIan is shot

And mind you, that this starter leg of the journey only gets us to Fort William, where just days ago we had a formal tea at Inverlochy Castle, and where - let's get serious – in 1690, *MacIan the MacDonald* came to pledge his kin's allegiance to *William of Orange*. And you now know how this turned out!

But Fort William is just the beginning of our journey home.

Next, we retrace our steps back through Glen Coe, headed for *The Bridge of Orchy*, the place mentioned earlier in the book, the place adjacent to the remote railroad stop hidden deep inside the Highlands.

We would stop at the Bridge of Orchy Inn for a much-needed rest, for a simple lunch, for a big beer and for a small cigar bought way back in Edinburg, kept for this moment.

Driving east through Glen Coe - a slow, long climb into higher and higher mountain sanctuaries - one eventually reaches the Bridge or Orchy, where, for centuries, the aforementioned Inn and Railroad Station greet all comers drifting through this remote corner of the earth.

Bridge and Hotel

Below, the western line cuts through the highlands on the way to Fort William and then up to Inverness. It stops at the Bridge of Orchy, where hikers come and go.

Our destination is the Bridge of Orchy pub.

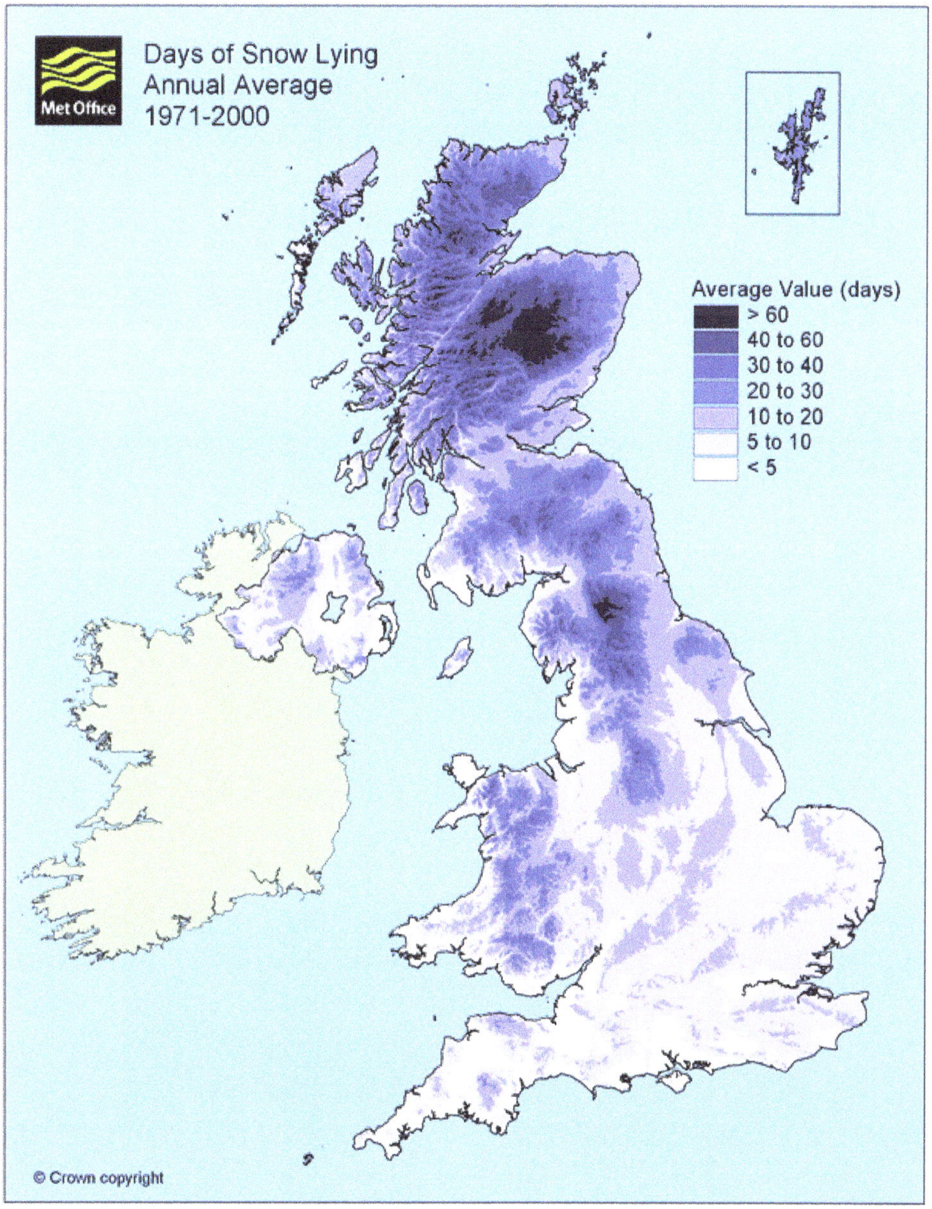

Inside, we are surely in Jacobean territory, with Gaelic accents as deep as any heard on the trip. These red/brown-haired lads with beards live here somewhere, though I have not seen any houses at all; they live in the glens, somehow out of sight.

Waiting for the food I walk around the pup looking at winter photographs of the deep snows that reach this upper region beyond Glen Coe.

The Western Line railroad at the Bridge of Orchy 1984.

And so, after all of these trips to Scotland, and after all of the stops made along the way, I just now realize that these locals, like the motorcycle lads I made eye contact with at Culloden Moor, carry no doubt of who they are: they are Scottish, 100% Scottish, and I am pleased to be with them.

Finishing lunch, I realize it's time to go home.

Outside I take the last photo...

At the Bridge of Orchy, deep in the Highlands, the ancient Scottish flag sits first, followed by the European Union flag, to which the Scottish consent, followed by the Union Jack.

Part - IV – Photos

"An Edinburg Pub – Author of Sherlock Holms",

"Annual Edinburg Summer Festival"

Edinburg Museum

"The Royal Mile – Edinburg"

Tara

Roommates – Joseph & Tara

Cody Near Glen Coe

Jolene & Tara on Skye

Joe on Skye

A Highland Romp – Near An Tellach

Lower Diabeg Cove

Bikers in Torridon

Joseph – Torridon House

Skye – Before Dinner

Laura – Skye Seaplane Air Field

Finally – Italian Food In Glasgow

Long Haul Travel

Back To Connecticut

Home & Dogs

Prestonfield "Fairy" Tree

Scotland

Copyright © 2010 By Joe Patrina

Well the Scottish air smells good today. Must've rained all night.
Winds are blow'n off the Irish Sea. Birds have dressed in white.
Standing here in awe. At everything we see.
Yea we've come back again. You're still here with me.

Well those souls out on the western islands. They let freedom ring.
Cold rain pour'n down forever. August takes everything.
Like to make their whiskey. Come rain or shine.
Flow'n like a river. Till the end of time.

Still talk'n 'bout the "Scottish Clearings". The people made to go
Sent 'em here to America. Them mountain men we know.
Look'n out for Nessie, yea. I wanna find her still.
I guess I'm still believ'n. Guess I always will.

Now the rain has ended. Spring lambs climb them hills.
The peat fires are burn'n. Do you love me still?

CHORUS:

I'll marry you with rings of bright water
That come to us from the heart of the sea
Carry you through rings of bright sunshine
That'll stay with us for eternity.

www.ingramcontent.com/pod-product-compliance
Lightning Source LLC
Chambersburg PA
CBHW061126070526
44584CB00033B/4234